YOU AND YOUR DREAMS

YOU AND YOUR DREAMS

Translated, compiled, and adapted by Mehr-Ali Kalami from the original writings of Hossein Kalami

VANTAGE PRESS
New York

FIRST EDITION

Published by Vantage Press, Inc.
516 West 34th Street, New York, New York 10001

Manufactured in the United States of America
ISBN: 0-533-09731-2

Library of Congress Catalog Card No.: 91-91074

0 9 8 7 6 5 4 3 2 1

CONTENTS

PREFACE

Since time immemorial, mankind has paid appreciable importance to the developments in the subconscious world. As a result, this has caused a continuous interest in the significance and the interpretation of dreams.

Hamid Ibn Qader (died 1946), the honored Syrian master, said: "Virtually all sane individuals are inwardly aware that there lie deep connections between a human being's activities in his conscious state and whatever he sees in his subconscious world. We can also say that certain impersonal forces over which we do not appear to have any sort of control are the ones that go to create a dream. These forces set to work once our conscious state gets deactivated (we sleep) to a certain extent, but not lapsing to a total or an absolute state of deactivation or deep sleep where the state of mind enters a temporary period of total blankness. The absolute state of deactivation renders the mental faculty fully blank during the subconscious state and hence prevents the formation of an image, whereas a semi-deactivated state is able to create the conditions that go to form a dream."

Hossein Kalami further wrote:

I have labored to reflect the interpretation of only those dreams that the 'masters' and I have deemed as interpretable. I advise my honored readers to try and find a befitting heading in the book which may be to a great extent linked or related to the subject matter of their dreams. Wherever possible, I have presented a 'note' for the dream discussed.

The Masters with whom Hossein met and communicated and learned from were:

Hamid Ibn Qader, a Syrian (1850–1946)
Karim Ibn Shafaq, a Syrian (1845–1944)
Jaafar Ibn Ibrahim, an Iraqi (___–1948)
Jassem Ibn Sarraf, an Iraqi (___–1946)
Mohammad Ibn Rasool, an Iraqi (___–1943)
Hakim Mohammad Jaafar Kuhestani, an Iranian (1848–1938)

Guru Baldev Singh Chaddah, Amritsar, India (___–1930)
Harish Chand Babu, Jullundur, India (___–___)
Maulana Faiz Ahmad, Lahore, India (now in Pakistan), (1850–1947)
Hakim Mehmet Rahmanoglou, Istanbul, Turkey (___–1947)
Hakim Burhan Beig, Ankara, Turkey (___–1946)

—Mehr-Ali Kalami

INTRODUCTION

Hossein Kalami (1871–1950) was born in a small village called Eishabad, some ten miles south of the desert city of Yazd, in central Iran. Hossein's father, Hassan (1840–1918), was an illiterate farmer who used to interpret dreams to the other villagers whenever the opportunity arose.

Hossein, after acquiring some rudimentary knowledge, studied the Koran and attended theology classes in Kerman (South-Central Iran) for a few years and at the Chahar Bagh Theology Center in Isfahan. In all, he studied theology for over eight years (1888–1896). At the same time, he showed a certain degree of interest in interpreting dreams.

Returning to Yazd, his interest deepened on the subject of dreams. In 1899, he began to make serious studies on this subject. In his manuscripts, mostly written on small pieces of paper, Hossein wrote:

> By the grace of the Almighty, in the year 1280 (Persian Calendar) which equals to 1901 of the Christian Calendar, I was some thirty years old and I decided to make extensive studies in analyzing dreams. Consequently, I had the opportunity to travel to several countries in the region. I travelled to several cities in India, some of which are now in Pakistan, Iraq, Syria and Turkey. There I met several honored masters who are later named to acquire their views and opinions concerning the hidden mysteries and the various significances of dreams.
>
> I have prepared these writings after more than four decades (1901–1945) of exhaustive consultations, research and exchange of views with the masters. The interpretations may not appear identical to those as expounded by other writers and scholars.

One may ask whether it is possible that dreams pertaining to one's development could be "commanded." A partially affirmative answer appears possible only through strenuous concentration and meditation, coupled with a relaxed state of mind prior to retirement at night. Spite, revenge, falsehood, and any other negated hopes must be totally cleared from the heart, mind, and spirit. Based on favorable conditions, it has been experienced in multitudes of instances that at least a faint message directly or indirectly manifests itself to the subject, thus giving him at minimum a hazy picture of the esoterics lying in store.

The profoundness of the impression that a certain dream bears upon an individual, such as an extremely delightful and satisfying event or one filled with "messages" of anguish, misery, and torment, essentially leaves that particular dream permanently pictured, perhaps till the last days of life on earth.

Hakim Burhan Beig, the Turkish expounder of the art of interpretation of dreams (died 1946), said:

> Time and again since centuries, it has been proved that a clearly recalled dream essentially signals messages either encouraging or otherwise and even signs of guidances on which we can accordingly alter our activities to fully utilize the possibilities seemingly awaiting us.
>
> Lest it be forgotten, or an incorrect conception be deduced, it is definitely the dreamer and no other person who finally infers as to whether the dream bears with it, if at all, any message or sign worthy of prophetic significance.

A controversy may arise in the mind of the reader as to why there exist differences of opinion among the expounders of dreams. This manuscript bases its interpretations purely on traditional beliefs and experiences and does not contradict in the least, whether directly or otherwise, the writings of other honored authors on this subject.

It should be added that the majority of dreams could be classified as unusual, strange, frightening, and even bizarre. Some could also be murky, unclear, and controversial. It is a fact that the conscious state stores within it certain developments of critical importance, both joyful and embarrassing, and refuses to part from such memories and unawaredly carries these thoughts and feelings all the way to the subconscious state where they "glow" into a full picture-like situation, thus giving the subject the possibility of more clearly understanding the supposed mysteries.

Excess anger, excitement, fright, despair, hopelessness, bitterness, hatred, affection, appreciation, joy, or hope over any development directly or indirectly related to a subject in a conscious state often manifests itself through a dream, more often of the "unusual" type. At the same time, a normal, calm, and a compromising mind, coupled with spiritual forces, can always be a factor to "see" a "normal" dream free of the unpleasant "extras" within it.

Within us, we feel aware of the reasons for the "types of dreams" we have. Our moral, mental, spiritual, and social situation, as well as our feelings, hatreds, and desires, are factors for a specific dream.

The honored reader is not asked to accept any of the interpretations in this manuscript as absolute fact, that something exact could materialize based on the interpretations. The subject of interpretation is not a perfect science. The writings have been reflected as a result of experiences accumulated through consultations and traditional beliefs. The reader is urged to rely more on his reason, logic, arguments, and understanding to derive an applicable result from this manuscript while trying to comprehend his subconscious state. Nevertheless, this manuscript solely reflects the belief of the writer and his findings. No individual is asked to believe or be addicted to the interpretations reflected in this manuscript as to be uniquely correct, incontestable, or a version claiming any divine inspiration or academic and spiritual pretensions.

—Hossein Kalami,
Yazd, Spring 1948

YOU AND YOUR DREAMS

Part One
A Dictionary of Dream Interpretation

A

ABA (a robe woven from the hair of goat or camel). Symbolizes comfort, honor, and respect.

a. You and aba: If you appear to have it on, it signifies comfort. It also means a modest and respectable life.

b. You are presenting it to someone: If you recognize the person to whom you are presenting it, the friendship between you and him will be strong. If you do not recognize him, it means that you will accidentally come across a new and useful friend.

c. Someone presents it to you: Such a dream foretells a timely help in the hour of need.

ABANDON. Any form of abandonment symbolizes a breakage in friendship and mental worries.

a. You abandon someone: Abandoning a child suggests a stormy period arising out of carelessness, while abandoning your spouse means an unrealistic approach to life. Abandoning a friend or animal underscores your emotional problems.

b. Someone abandons you: If you are abandoned by your parents or spouse, it foretells deep misunderstandings within the family.

ABBEY. For centuries this dream has come to symbolize an end to emotional conflicts. It is widely believed that peace and calm follow such a dream.

a. You see an abbey: Such a dream asks you not to despair but to accept the challenges of life with calm. But if you appear to be inside an abbey, it means a general transformation, for the better will follow soon regardless of your present situation, but only if you appear sitting or standing idly.

b. You find yourself with a woman inside an abbey: If you recognize the woman with whom you are, it suggests a female person will ultimately help you. If you are unmarried and you recognize the woman, it suggests a true romance will come along quite soon. If you are already married, it underscores the strong bonds between you and your spouse.

c. You are eating inside an abbey: If you appear eating alone, it is an unmistakable sign of the end of bitter days; if with someone, it suggests friends and acquaintances will hasten to your help at the hour of need.

d. You appear to be writing inside an abbey: If presenting an application for any specific request, it is a sure sign that there will be at least a partial positive response to it. If a writer by profession, it means success in this field.

ABBOT. A very propitious dream, signifying prosperity and good health.

a. He is lecturing you: Such a dream suggests that within the next few days you will benefit from the admonishments of a person, which will ultimately change your way of life for the better.

b. You are speaking to him: Such a dream means that you will gain the confidence of those around you; and if in business, you will have further prosperity.

c. He is giving you something: If the abbot gives you anything, worthless or otherwise, it suggests you will regain your lost health and improve emotionally. If you appear to be giving him something, it means health and wealth are yours.

ABDOMEN. Abdomen symbolizes health. Depending on its situation, an interpretation can be had.

a. You appear wounded in the region of the abdomen: Such a dream suggests that you will undergo a short period of illness unless you seek professional guidance. If you dream of having healed scars on it, it means you will be able to prevent any general setback due to your own cautious ways of life.

b. You see blood dripping from your abdomen: If the blood appears to be "too much," it must be considered as an organic dream with no prophetic significance, but if there is a little amount of blood dripping, it means your sorrows in general will increase unless you move quick enough. An abdomen that appears to be in a normal state underlines the fact that you pay the required attention to your health. It also means a modest and a careful person.

ABYSS. An abyss or any bottomless pit symbolizes dangers, which may manifest at later stages. It also symbolizes unbearable anguish chiefly arising due to one's own faults and carelessness.

a. You are standing over or looking down an abyss: Such a dream forebodes dangers lurking around. It is also a warning to replan your objectives in life or face disproportional consequences. If you manage to have a more sagacious approach to your daily life, things could ameliorate, though in the distant future.

b. You have fallen into an abyss: Such a dream means simply "Crime does not pay." The simple interpretation here is that you have followed an unlawful, incorrect, and sinful life so far devoid of respect for the law and feelings for mankind in general. Hence, having fallen into an abyss is none other than repayment for your crimes and misdeeds.

ACCIDENT. An accident in one's dream symbolizes the possibilities of danger.

a. You see an accident: If the accident involves an animal-drawn vehicle, it is a warning not to undertake any business risks until you are certain of a good result. If the animal appears hurt or any person is hurt, it strengthens the suggestion that you are heading for a financial loss. If two mechanically powered vehicles are seen in the accident, it betokens an unforeseen mishap affecting your domestic life.

5

b. You are involved in an accident: Such a dream asks you to be extremely careful in what you plan and where you go. If you appear to be in a motor vehicle or a train that is involved in the accident, it means that you must postpone any business journey.

ACCOUNTANT. An accountant in one's dream symbolizes justice to your labors in life. Depending on the situation, several interpretations can be made.

a. You and the accountant: If the accountant summons you and you feel guilty, it means you are hiding certain facts that could lead to worries. If you ask to see the accountant for business reasons, it means you will make your own means of livelihood, perhaps through a small business that will turn out to be modestly successful. If you find yourself to be arguing with the accountant, it means several matters, both business and domestic, need to be reviewed. If you just happen to see the accountant whom you recognize, it means encouragement to your affairs in general. If someone introduces you to an accountant, it means that destiny appears to favor you, such that you will arrive at your modest goals earlier than you predict.

b. You are an accountant: A good dream suggesting your honest behavior will finally lead you to better days as a result of the increase of confidence the society will have in you. It also means justice to your labors.

ACNE (pimples on the face). Acne, spots or pimples on the face, symbolizes hardships and problems arising out of jealousy.

a. You and acne: If you find yourself with acne, and you do not have acne in reality, it means certain individuals whom you have wrongly trusted as friends will betray you. Correct your ways in life so that their acts will not have any negative effects on you in front of the law. If you really do have acne and dream of it time to time, it suggests your honesty, as you do not have anything to hide.

b. Others have acne: Whether they have it in true life or not, the presence of any person with acne, other than your own siblings and

6

parents, suggests deep jealousy towards you. Pursue your life such that undesired feelings towards you shall cease.

ACQUITTAL. Acquittal in one's dream symbolizes better times in the future. Being acquitted or found innocent also signifies that your friends have been wrong in their judgments of you.

a. You are acquitted by your friends: Such a dream means that you will enter into a new period of life full of calm and tranquillity. You will also earn the respect and confidence of others.

b. You are acquitted of any wrongdoing by the law: Such a dream suggests a "comedy of misunderstanding" between you and your family members, but they will finally come to respect you.

c. You acquit others: Forgiving and acquitting others for any misunderstanding or even a wrongdoing suggests you are un-awaredly acquiring spiritual gains.

ADMIRATION. Admiration for an object or an individual in one's dream symbolizes contentment and calm within you.

a. You admire: If you admire an object either of artistic value or otherwise, it suggests that either you are undergoing a period of calm and tranquillity or in the near future you will arrive at your modest goals. If you appear to admire a man, it means you have the qualities to develop your personality and if you happen to admire a woman, it strongly suggests your satisfaction with your family members, especially with your spouse and children.

b. Others admire you: Such a dream means that your presence has proved beneficial to the society. It also means that you are continuing to climb the ladder of luck.

AIRPLANE (any flying object). An airplane symbolizes both favorable as well as unfavorable developments. Depending on the situation of the aircraft and you, several interpretations can be derived.

a. You see an airplane: If the aircraft appears to be flying low, it underscores your contented philosophy in life. If it appears to be flying at a high altitude, you must consider your immediate situation and accordingly choose any one of the interpretations that appear more applicable to you:

- If employed or following a lawful profession, it suggests a promotion.
- If you are in business, it suggests appreciable gains.
- If unemployed but with positive talents, it suggests an employment opportunity in the near future.
- If indulging in a negative profession, it means a sudden upward surge in your activities to be accompanied by a sudden fall, perhaps ending in a legal suit against you.
- If virtuous and expecting an answer to your needs or requirements, a positive and pleasant response is foretold.
- If you see an aircraft taxi on the runway, it is a sign of encouragement to pursue your goals, since they appear to be planned in the right direction.
- An aircraft taking off means you have every right to believe in your just cause, which will ultimately take you to your goals.

b. You are in an airplane: If flying in an airplane, it means absolute satisfaction to your labors in life. If seated at the airport in an airplane that is just about to depart, it suggests that very soon you will have a short and a fruitful journey. If the airplane appears to taxi with you seated within, it means you can have confidence in your friends. If the airplane appears to be falling with you inside it, it suggests losses due to your indecisions and nervous disposition. But if the craft appears to regain its bearings, it indicates a temporary setback in business and domestic affairs, but with a return to normalcy at a later period.

c. A crashed airplane: If you see a crashed airplane from a distance, it denotes undesired indulgences will lead you to sorrow, unless you move fast enough to prevent losses by careful planning. If you happen to be very near the wreckage, it signifies your present situation is not too satisfying due to constant problems created by unscrupulous persons around you.

d. You pilot an airplane: An exceptionally good dream foretelling your ability or perhaps hidden talents within you that if exploited well could lead to better days. If you happen to be near or even talking to the pilot of the airplane, it suggests the possibility of lifting off from dark and unpleasant days.

ALMS. Depending on your situation, such a dream signifies health, wealth, and happiness.

a. You are giving alms: If you already have a good financial situation and appear to be giving alms to the needy, you will further prosper. If you are planning to embark on a business trip, you are assured of success. If you plan to marry, a successful marriage and a good partner await you. In short, such a dream signifies health, wealth, and happiness.

b. You are receiving alms: This does not mean that misfortune has afflicted you, since giving alms is attributed to those who have reached the threshold of prosperity, while those receiving alms are identified as individuals on the verge of getting off the ground. Hence, receiving alms in a way assures that you are taking off in the right direction.

ALTAR (any altar where one prays). A dream signifying happiness or unhappiness depending on the situation.

a. You are facing the altar and praying: If you are in good spirits, it signifies bounty and happiness are yours in the near future. This is such, since you are thanking the Creator for what you have received.

b. You appear unhappy while at the altar: If you are unhappy at the altar, it denotes affliction and could herald a difficult period . . . perhaps losing a near and a dear one.

ANCHOR. Depending on the situation of the anchor, the significance of the dream could be interpreted as good or bad.

a. You see an anchor on land: Seeing an anchor lying on land signifies your activities are heading for a standstill. It also means difficult days are looming ahead. It also means you are refusing to face the realities of life. But if a rope or chain appears tied to the anchor, it means that there are hopes that the anchor (here, meaning your perseverance) will be again utilized by a boat, which translates that your full possibilities will be exploited through your own will. Hence, the rope or the chain attached makes the vast difference.

b. You see an anchor in the water: If the anchor appears attached to a boat and is seen well, it means that certain problems for which you are personally responsible have slowed down your progress. Nevertheless the unfavorable period will end soon through your own desires. But if a stray anchor simply appears to be resting on the bed of the water, it means bad news often related to sickness and death in the family.

c. A ship lowering its anchor: If the water appears clear and you can see the anchor being lowered, it means that there are fairly good chances for you to further prosper in life, but if the water appears murky, it denotes that forces appear to be against you for the moment. An anchor seen being pulled up from the seabed denotes immense chances and opportunities to explore your talents, only if directed towards constructive acts.

ANGEL. An angel's presence symbolizes happiness.

a. You see an angel: Since an angel's features are only conceived as a "female with wings, usually with a bugle or a spear," it is but natural that something in dream seen to resemble such a "being" is considered an angel. If seen, it means that you will realize the major part of your goals in life. If married, you will have a perfect married life; if unmarried, you will have a decent and a trustworthy partner.

b. An angel talks with you or comes near you: In case you are sick or afflicted, you will recover; in case you are poverty-stricken, you will have better days.

c. The angel scolds or chides you: Such a dream warns you to be more cautious towards your relations with friends and others around you. Exercise restraint over your emotions.

ANXIETY. Anxiety in dream does not necessarily foretell unhappiness, as it implies.

a. You appear anxious: Such a state in your dream denotes the fact that you are anxiously awaiting a sudden change for the better in your life. It also means that you are not willing to reconsider any changes to your plans whatever the outcome may be. Anxiety also signifies considerable amelioration of your worries. Here, the simple advice is not to over-exaggerate your woes in your conscious state, since things appear to favor you for the moment.

b. Others in your presence appear to be anxious: This means that you will attain a respectable and a responsible position in life where you will be in a situation to help and guide others towards a better life.

ARGUMENT. Depending on the situation and with whom you have an argument, an interpretation can be had.

a. You argue: If it is a heated argument with another man, it suggests a temporary setback in your professional activities. But since you appear to argue defiantly, it means you have the ability to defend yourself and hence any adverse effects to your activities will be less. If you appear to argue with any woman, it indicates a degree of misunderstanding with your spouse (if married) or a temporary break with your future partner.

b. You argue with your parents: A dream strongly warning you to alter your behavior or face the results, which may not be too favorable.

ARMY. A dream symbolizing favorable as well as unfavorable developments. Depending on the situation of the army, several interpretations can be had. Listed below are various interpretations:

a. An assembled army group, well dressed with arms, but not

11

intended to go to battle: Such a dream signifies an imminent meeting with a well-paced military figure whose presence will ultimately mean a fundamental change in your life.

b. An army shabbily dressed, tired and retreating but not defeated: This signifies an imminent loss of property or an unexpected loss in your financial activities. In case the soldiers appear to be wounded and bandaged or on stretchers, it forebodes a terrible mishap in the family often to be related to a series of fatal accidents or illnesses.

c. An army parading as if in some ceremony: Such a dream heralds a possible celebration by you or someone within your family. It could also mean the end of a bitter period for you personally. If the army parading has arms, it signifies a significant prosperity and adds to the reason of a celebration.

d. An army that appears to have retreated in defeat: Such a dream does not necessarily spell defeat for you; on the contrary, it signifies a fundamental change in your life through your own efforts, which will be for the better. The logic is an army that has retreated in defeat is bound to again reorganize itself and prepare for another shot at victory with greater zeal. For you, failure, if any, will be short and temporary.

e. An army group welcoming you towards them: Such a dream is said to be an inspiration to you to try to overcome your problems. Your problems, although negligible, appear unbearable to you.

f. An army group relaxing or "at ease": This suggests the definite need to rest to overcome mental and physical exhaustion.

g. You see a heavily armed army group awaiting battle orders: Such a dream warns you to be on guard against jealous individuals around you.

h. One army is pitched against the other in combat: Such a dream often indicates a period of anxiety. It also underscores your adamant nature and your refusal to face the bitter facts of life. If there is a sudden "cease fire" or a halt to the fighting, friends and relatives will intervene to help you in your difficult situation.

ARREST. Arrest of any kind in a dream does not necessarily symbolize the dreamer's possible detention in his conscious life. Many "masters" have interpreted "arrest" as a sign of being safe and away from harm. A unique example of a dream signifying the contrary.

a. You are arrested: If you are just arrested and not taken into custody, it suggests you will singlehandedly extricate yourself from your domestic entanglements. If you are experiencing a financial setback, your own honest efforts will help you. But if you appear to be remanded in custody, it means not only you will triumph over your difficulties very soon, but that you will also be safe from any violent developments.

ARROW. An arrow symbolizes a tense period marked with unhappiness.

a. You are shooting an arrow: Such a dream underlines your unhappy, isolated, and despairing situation. Nervousness appears to have had an upper hand on you and you appear hopeless. Think and plan carefully . . . control your anger and meditate.

b. You are being or have been shot by an arrow: Such a dream warns you of the consequences of your erratic behavior, which will cause you great sufferings and loss. Admonishments from the elders will greatly help you rid yourself of your present situation.

ASH. Ash symbolizes destruction and end to a specific cycle in life. Several interpretations are listed:

a. You see ash: If you see ash around you, it means your life's goal will be ultimately achieved, in the sense that fruitage will begin in the latter part of your life.

b. You see ash on your body: Such a dream signifies the end of a particular cycle in life. If you are a merchant, you will change your profession and so on. But it does not conclude that on changing your trade you will commence another lifestyle where you will have more riches or prosperity. It denotes a total change, where you will exchange your present material holdings for spiritual gains. Even if you do not have any material holdings, you will achieve spiritual wealth.

ASSASSIN. An assassin in one's dream symbolizes bad tidings. As such, it is considered an unfavorable dream.

a. You and an assassin: If the assassin nears you and threatens you but does no harm to you, it signals an impending array of problems that may strongly affect your daily life. It may also mean an accident or illness, often grave. Such a dream also suggests financial loss if you intend to enter any business deal. Refrain from travel and business undertakings for at least a week.

b. The assassin stabs you and escapes: Such a dream forebodes quarrels, which may turn violent, with you being wounded. If you see a lot of blood, the dream is devoid of any prophetic significance, but if you see no blood, dangers to your life or some form of terrible development is in store for you. Meditation and calm will ultimately eliminate any harm to you.

B

BABY (newly born). A newly born baby is an auspicious sign, symbolizing good health, success, and happiness.

a. You see a baby: A newly born baby symbolizes success and prosperity in all your affairs. In business, love, and general affairs, you will meet one success after another. A crying baby denotes a new life and a new beginning.

b. You see a woman holding a baby: If you are unmarried, such a dream foretells a marriage in the near future. If married, it suggests a complete harmony with your spouse. If you see a man holding a baby, petty misunderstandings will create uneasiness within the family. If married and you see such a dream, practice restraint. But

14

if a married couple happen to be near their baby, it denotes happiness. If you are unmarried, it speaks of a successful marriage. If you are sick and see such a dream, speedy recovery is foretold.

c. **You see a dead baby:** A dead baby signifies absolute recklessness and irresponsibility on your part, which may often lead to increased worries and marital problems. It also reflects your indifference towards your own life.

BAG. A bag symbolizes favorable developments usually associated with financial gains.

a. **You see a bag:** If the bag is closed and appears lying on the floor or ground, it is an encouraging sign to go ahead with any small business project that you may have. If the bag appears on a table, bed, or chair, it foretells sudden riches through inheritance.

b. **You hold a bag in your hand:** Whether empty or full, it denotes a sudden change for the better, which would have with it a financial gain. If you appear to hold a bag with money or some worthy thing inside it under your arm, it suggests a satisfying end to your projects or aspirations. If you are employed or in business, it means money from a source you least expected.

BAKER. A baker in one's dream symbolizes the arrival of good news and satisfactory results to labors.

a. **You and a baker:** If you happen to see your local baker in the street, it is a good sign, assuring the fruition of your labors. If you see him in the bakery, the promise of good results to your labors is even stronger. If you see him working with the dough, it means very good news is on its way, perhaps something that will change the course of your life. Giving the baker something means surprise news, often pleasant, while receiving something from him simply means "good luck is just around the corner." Any argument with a baker means a sudden mishap due to sheer negligence. If you dream you are a baker, it means you will be offered a new employment opportunity that will greatly satisfy you.

15

BALCONY. Depending on your situation vis-à-vis the balcony, an interpretation can be had.

a. You are on the balcony: If you appear alone on the balcony, it suggests a considerable promotion to your personal status in life due to your wisdom and care. If you happen to be either with friends or family members, it means you will further gain the confidence of those around you and the society in general. If you appear on the balcony with your business partner, it means an unexpected gain in your business dealings.

b. You have fallen down from a balcony: If you happen to fall from the balcony, it suggests excesses and undesired extravagances will ultimately create loss or a setback. If the balcony happens to fall with you, the above negative effects will be more. It also underscores your corrupt and unlawful methods in handling business affairs. It has been widely suggested that it is often the corrupt and unscrupulous businessmen and professional swindlers who dream of falling with the balcony.

BALD. Baldness symbolizes a general loss. Depending on the dreamer's situation, an interpretation can be had. An unfavorable dream indeed.

a. You and baldness: If you (a man) dream of being bald (while you are not bald in the conscious state), it foretells losses and worries arising out of your untoward activities, perhaps fraud and hypocrisy. If you are really bald and see your bald head, it is a sign asking you to refrain from any wrongful indulgences, which may cost you dearly. If you (a woman) dream of becoming bald, it speaks of temptations within you to indulge in any act that may bring you wealth.

b. You see bald persons: If you happen to see several bald women around you, it suggests you are gradually slipping into the world of negative acts. If you see several bald men around you, it is a warning to be alert and careful in your dealings.

BANDITS. Bandits in a dream symbolize your reckless behavior. It also symbolizes your reluctance to develop your life in general.

a. You and bandits: If you see bandits who do not harm you, it is just a warning that disaster awaits you unless you move fast enough to prevent it. But if the bandits appear to attack you or your property and you appear helpless, it suggests the results of your past activities will cost you a lot. If you appear to confront them or even frighten them away, it is a hopeful sign, denoting a last-minute change within your ways of life will prevent a catastrophic situation for you and your family.

b. You are a bandit: Such a dream underscores your criminal intentions. If you happen to be robbing, attacking, or burning a place, it means evil has finally gained the upper hand on you. Meditation coupled with prayers will essentially help you overcome the undesired temptations within you.

BANQUET. A banquet in one's dream symbolizes future prosperity and good health.

a. You are present at a banquet: Such a dream means you will very soon witness the fruits of your labors. If you are an invitee and alone, it means you will very soon solve your immediate problems alone. If accompanied by someone, it is a good sign, indicating a joint business venture with a trustworthy person.

b. You give a banquet: This is considered a rare dream usually seen by philanthropic persons. If you are young, you will possibly inherit a large fortune, while if already engaged in business, it suggests further prosperity coupled with good health.

BARBER. A barber's presence in one's dream symbolizes petty quarrels, delay in realization of one's project, and a brief period of financial problems. His presence is considered ominous in a dream.

a. You and a barber: A barber outside his shop symbolizes hypocrisy, while if he is seen idle within his place of work, it means a tense period within the family appears to begin due to misunderstandings.

If the barber appears to be cutting your hair, it means you are yourself the architect of your present problems, although you blame others. It also means a period marked by quarrels and general disappointment in life. If accidentally all your hair appears cut or shaved, it means all outstanding misunderstandings, if any, will be settled to the satisfaction of all. If you ask the barber to stop cutting your hair or he suddenly stops doing so, it means your problems, whatever they are, will be brief. It also means you will arrive at your desires, however, with a delay.

b. You are a barber: An unfavorable dream ultimately meaning that you will not mind indulging in unlawful means to get your desires. It also means abasement in general, especially where your general life is concerned.

BASKET. Depending on the size and the situation of the basket, an interpretation can be had. Usually a basket is deemed to be associated with financial activities.

a. You and a basket: If the basket appears quite large, has holes in it, and is empty, it is a direct message advocating care and reticence where your business or financial activities are concerned. If there is at least one object in it, whether worthy or otherwise, it means the degree of loss could be lessened or even averted through wise counsel. If the basket appears covered and you find it to be empty within, you are the victim of fraud by those whom you consider to be friends. A small basket with similar description means financial problems, if any, will not greatly damage your life. If the basket appears to be well knit, empty, without any holes, and of any size, it means you will arrive at your modest goals, but with a struggle. If full with anything, it symbolizes a period of plenty with happiness and tranquillity.

BASTARD (any illegitimate person). A bastard signifies sorrows and miseries. In short, just as it is considered as an ominous sign to see a bastard in the conscious state, similarly in a dream too, the bastard's presence (only if you are sure that he is one) forebodes nothing but problems. Vis-à-vis his presence, his actions, and what he says, several other significances can be had.

18

a. You and a bastard: If the bastard appears to be walking or sitting nearby and you recognize him but do not exchange any form of greetings, it means that you have the ability to shun vice, but if he approaches you and greets you and you answer him, it means that you are getting weak morally. If you refuse to answer him and ignore him, it is a sign that you cannot be tricked easily into committing any unlawful acts. If the bastard appears with his mother (since a bastard seldom knows his father's identity, he is usually with his mother till his early twenties. It is widely believed that since his mother may have been of loose character as a result of having a bastard child, she could not be expected to give any proper upbringing to her illegitimate child) and if they appear to be arguing with each other, it is a direct message to you to be practical, studious, hard-working, and honest in order to gain the maximum benefits of your labor. If they appear to be exchanging pleasantries, it means there are conspiracies against you by persons whom you will very soon recognize.

If a bastard gives you good news or encouraging advice, it indicates a loss and miseries unless you rush to find the facts behind your problems. On the contrary, if the bastard gives you bad news or prophesizes bad news and developments for you, it is a sure sign of prosperity and calm. If you argue, quarrel, or ask a bastard to leave your premises, it is a good sign, ridding yourself of bad acquaintances. If you (the mother of a bastard child) dream of seeing him or her, it is a certain sign that you will continue to tread the same shameful path that you have been doing for the past years and that nothing but prison life awaits you for your future. Rarely does a mother of a bastard see her child or children. Such a dream occurs to a mother who is hopelessly doomed to a life of committing fraud and crimes.

BATH. Taking a bath in one's dream symbolizes the cleansing of worries, whether financial or domestic. Depending on the water and your situation while taking a bath, an interpretation can be had.

a. You take a bath: If you appear to take a bath in a flowing water, it strongly suggests the immediate elimination of your major problems, provided the water you "see" appears clean. If the water appears murky or muddy, it means the stress that you have gained through such worries will slightly lessen. Taking a bath in a "hot tub" signifies a satisfying result to your domestic problems. If another person appears to give you a bath, it implies encouragements from friends that will greatly ameliorate your situation in life. Taking a bath "with your clothes on" reflects the reckless behavior you insist on following.

b. You see others take a bath: Seeing several people, whether men or women, take a bath either in a pond, a river, or a general public bath means things in general appear to change for you. However, although not for the best, at least for the better.

BEANS. Beans in one's dream symbolize hardships, quarrels, and even sickness. At the same time, depending on the quality of the beans seen, favorable interpretations can also follow:

a. You and beans: Fresh beans of any type and color either in the vegetable patch or ready to be cooked symbolize success in business, a period of calm and tranquillity, and general satisfaction in life. Eating uncooked fresh beans foretells good health, and for those ailing a general recovery. Eating them cooked speaks of your care in daily affairs of life. Seeing dried beans suggests a sickness, which could worsen unless you consult a specialist. Eating them cooked signifies a bleak financial situation while serving them to others around you means there are possibilities that you will quarrel with your friends and neighbors over petty matters. Buying dried beans speaks of acute financial problems.

BEARD. A beard has favorable as well as unfavorable significances in one's dream. Depending on the type of beard and the situation of the dreamer, interpretations can be had.

a. You and a beard: If you see a person with a short beard, it denotes a temporary general success in life only to revert at a later period. If the beard appears long and flowing, it denotes success with more stability. If you see a person whom you recognize and who does not have a beard but appears bearded in the dream, it suggests deceit and fraud will engulf your later life unless you rush to mend your ways in life. If you have a beard and dream of it, it means there appears to be less or virtually no change in your life for the moment.

But if you do not have a beard and dream of being bearded, it means a lawsuit may arise against you on charges of fraud. If you see a woman with a beard, it strongly underscores your tendencies towards a life filled with sin and crime.

BED. A bed in one's dream symbolizes idleness, sickness, and financial setbacks.

a. You and a bed: Just seeing a bed either near or from a distance suggests a short period marked with unhappiness. If you appear to be just resting on a bed, it means there are possibilities to embark on a new project without any danger. But if you appear to be on a bed with a blanket on you, it foretells sickness, which may not be acute. If you appear sitting on a bed, it foretells a fairly long period of financial setbacks with unemployment. Buying a bed foretells the imminent arrival of good news. If you are asked to lie down or sit on a bed by anyone, it indicates a well-earned rest after a successful business deal. It may also signal a change for the better in your life. If unmarried, there appears a prospect for a good spouse.

BEGGAR. Depending on the situation, a beggar in one's dream symbolizes both favorable as well as unfavorable developments.

a. You see a beggar: A warning of impending bad news unless you move fast enough to control your emotions. If the beggar approaches you not to beg but to speak, it means unhappy days are ahead. But if the beggar begs and you give him something, it suggests you are about to receive unexpected financial help from a quarter you least expect. Such a dream also spells a general prosperity all of a sudden. If you refuse to give the beggar anything, it means you will continue to lead the same life that you are presently leading.

b. You are a beggar: A dream for those on the verge of prosperity. If you dream you are in rags and in misery, it means you are encouraged to go ahead with whatever plans you have, for they appear to be lawful and well planned. Be it business, travel, or domestic, success is yours.

c. A beggar presents you with something: This is an unfavorable dream. Due to your arrogance, you will have a heavy fall. Take care of your health and your dealings with friends, acquaintances, business partners, or co-workers. If self-employed postpone any new ventures for the time being.

BELL. A bell symbolizes good news.

a. You see a bell: Such a dream symbolizes better times for the future. It also underscores your perseverance towards a better standard of life. If you have any plans, undertake them with utmost care.

b. You hear a bell ringing: This symbolizes that your projects have been crowned with success even though you are unaware of it. In short, you will be rewarded more than you expect. A church bell, however, signifies sad news.

c. You strike a bell: It indicates your full satisfaction with life. It also means a happy married life. For those unmarried it foretells a sudden meeting with your future partner in life.

BICYCLE. A bicycle symbolizes awareness and unawareness of thoughts. Depending on the situation of the bicycle and you, an interpretation can be had.

a. You see a bicycle: Just seeing a bicycle means you are not sure of what you are doing. It also denotes a fickle nature.

b. You are riding a bicycle: Such a dream means you are well aware of your actions, but it does not definitely denote success to your labors. Nevertheless, it does not forebode any loss.

c. You are presented with a bicycle: Such a dream means you can count on your friends for a nominal assistance. It also means your decisive actions are necessary to arrive at a satisfying result, as you cannot wait for nature to take its own course.

BIRTH. A birth in one's dream symbolizes the commencement of a new and fruitful cycle in the dreamer's life.

a. You witness a birth: Such a dream means a sudden transformation (for the better) awaits you. It also means (in case you are married) your spouse and children will have a good future, and if employed, you can expect a promotion or a better employment opportunity.

b. You hear of a birth: If it concerns the family, it is a good omen signifying the resolution of your financial problems. If it is outside the family, it indicates a general amelioration in your life.

BLANKET. A blanket symbolizes a cautious approach to life and the desire to prevent any untoward development.

a. You sit on a blanket: Sitting on a blanket means you are not fully utilizing your talents or abilities to gain the fruits of life. It also means you tend to be indifferent to the opportunities provided.

b. You buy a blanket: Buying a blanket means you are sincerely interested in bettering your situation. It also strongly underlines your cautious approach to life where health and financial affairs are concerned.

c. You are presented a blanket: Such a dream means that your friends and family members have respect for you and desire your benefit.

d. You present a blanket to others: Presenting a blanket to others than your immediate family members indicates you will achieve the larger part of your desires in life where you will be in a position to offer help and protection to others.

BLIND. Blindness in a dream symbolizes utter stupidity and recklessness, often leading to an unpleasant situation and disappointments.

a. You see a blind person: This is a warning to mend your ways. It is also a signal that it is time to awaken from your sleep in life. Seeing a blind person also foretells a sudden financial downfall.

b. You see someone leading a blind person: Such a dream indicates a friend or a family member will eventually assist you to extricate yourself from your present problems through wise counsel.

c. **You are blind:** Such a dream warns you to take great care in your daily affairs. It also warns you to select your friends well and be more prudent in your mind.

BOAT (a rowboat). A boat signifies hope and success.

a. **You see a boat:** Just seeing a boat on a calm water means that there are good opportunities to achieve your goals. If the waters appear choppy, it means efforts have to be made. In general, a boat is a symbol of hope.

b. **You are in a boat:** If alone, your own efforts will lead you to success. If with friends or family members, it means they will play a major role in your success. Their presence also means they have confidence in you.

BONES. Bones in one's dream are often said to be associated with a nervous disposition, loss, and sickness.

a. **You see human bones:** Such a dream means you will lose a very good friend as a result of your unbearable attitude. If you see bones scattered all over, it underscores your nervous behavior where you tend to accuse people. If the bones appear to be piled up, it suggests sickness.

b. **You see animal bones:** Animal bones signify financial loss and domestic problems. If you leave the place out of fright or disgust, there is no prophetic significance to the dream.

c. **You come across unidentified bones:** Such a dream reflects your violent temper. It also spells dangers of quarrels and misunderstandings within the family. For those married, a bitter disagreement is not ruled out.

d. **You are presented with bones:** Such a dream forebodes immense financial losses. It also means your friends will progressively leave you due to your erratic behavior.

BOOKS. A book symbolizes success and other favorable developments.

a. You see one or more books: Just seeing one book or more signifies the fact that you have the required potentials within you to prosper.

b. You buy a book: Buying a book is a sign of encouragement to go ahead with your plans. It is also a sign of promise of success to your modest wishes in life.

c. You are presented with a book: Whether new or old, a book presented to you is a reminder that you have the confidence of friends. It also means that you will receive every possible help from them.

d. You are reading a book: This means you will probably arrive at your goals alone. It also suggests success in any legal entanglement. If you appear to be reading a handwritten book with an attractive cover or a newly printed book, it is a sign of financial gains. But if the book appears shabby or falling apart, it is a sign of impending mental worries.

BOTTLE. The significance of a bottle in dream depends on its situation such as empty, full, broken, large, small, its contents and even color. As such, it symbolizes prosperity as well as setbacks.

a. You see a large empty bottle: A large empty bottle signifies your "easy going" ways in life, which could eventually have a general impact on your life. It also underlines your lazy and dreamy nature.

b. You see a small bottle: A small empty bottle reflects your fickle nature. Although at times you tend to be more realistic and serious, still lack of determination on your part appears to get the best of you.

c. You see a bottle that is full of wine, water, juice, or any other potable liquid. A full bottle foretells prosperity and continued good health. It also means a general amelioration where domestic and financial matters are concerned. It also means prosperity in business. The larger the bottle the stronger the possibilities appear and otherwise in case the bottle is small. The lighter the color the better is the prophecy.

d. You see a bottle full of perfume: Such a dream foretells a happy married life.

e. You see a broken bottle: A broken bottle foretells a financial loss. If there are several broken bottles, it increases the significance of loss.

f. You are presented with a bottle: Irrespective of its size and color and if it holds some liquid in it, there is every reason for you to depend on your friends. If the bottle is empty, it is a warning to stop depending on those around you.

BOX. A box can be a harbinger of good as well as bad news. Depending on the situation of the box and you, several interpretations can be had. The size and color of the box has no prophetic significance.

a. You see a box: Whether metal or wooden, if the box appears closed, it indicates you will have difficulties making decisions. If the box is open and contains anything, it is an encouragement to go ahead with your plans, which will be crowned with success. If open and empty, it signifies false promises. It also forebodes unhappy news.

b. You are opening a box: Opening a box in a dream underscores the inner perseverance within you. If you find difficulty in opening it, you will be faced with temporary hardships, but if you manage to open it, you are assured of at least a partial success in your endeavors.

c. You are presented with a box: Regardless of its size, a box presented to you is a harbinger of good luck in almost every sphere of your life.

d. You break open a box with an instrument: Breaking open a box in one's dream signifies unearthing a development that was so far a secret for you. It also foretells the lessening or the virtual elimination of conspiracies against you. It also means you will have new friendships much better than those you plan or have already disowned.

BOY. A boy symbolizes good health and a new beginning in life.

a. You see a boy: Such a dream symbolizes vitality, definite recovery from illness, and a sudden change in your life, which will chiefly be for the better.

b. You see boys playing: A favorable sign, indicating an end to a difficult period. It also means an end to domestic and financial problems.

c. You see boys quarreling: A direct warning to immediately stop your extravagant ways in life and to heed the advice of the elders. Such a dream also reflects your rashness and lack of ability to use your logic to solve simple problems. If one or more of the boys appear injured, it means utmost care is advocated in dealing with your day-to-day affairs.

BREAD. Bread symbolizes a good period with sufficient riches and good health.

a. You see bread: Seeing bread in a dream, regardless of its size and color, often foretells the end of an unhappy period. It is also a sign of moral encouragement. The quantity of the bread reflects the degree of happiness you will receive. Stale bread signifies your failure in the past to utilize the several chances and opportunities that were available to you.

b. You are buying bread: Buying bread signifies the possibilities of a financial prosperity. It also means more wealth than you can expect. Distributing bread to the needy underscores your philanthropic nature.

c. You are eating bread: Such a dream means good health with a long life is yours. If you are sick, you will appreciably recover.

d. You are presented with bread: Bread presented to you by an elderly person denotes an unexpected inheritance. If it is given to you by a young man, it signals the immediate exit from a bad financial situation. If a young woman presents you with bread, you can expect a happy married life.

e. You are making bread: The general belief of the "masters" is that baking or making bread symbolizes your ability to continuedly make a decent living and to help those in distress.

f. You are throwing away bread: Such a dream denotes domestic and financial problems, heated arguments often ending in violence. Such a dream also forebodes separation and even divorce in the family. It also presages sad news; perhaps a death in the family.

BREAST. A woman's breast symbolizes strength, vitality, courage, and the will to overcome one's hardships.

a. You (a man) and woman's breasts: If the woman appears bare-breasted, it means you will continue to enjoy good health. If ailing with minor sickness, you will recover within a week. If you happen to touch her breasts, it is an unmistakable sign of courage gathering within you to challenge the hardships of life tormenting you. If the breasts appear swollen with milk, it is a definite sign of success to any one of your projects within forty days. Seeing a woman breast-feed her baby is a good sign, denoting a gradual strengthening of your will power. A wounded or a disfigured breast is a harbinger of a temporary period of setbacks but without any acute effects on your health or general situation.

b. You (a man) develop breasts: This means you have the potentials within you to embark on a more constructive project in life. Your success will, however, depend on your perseverance.

BRIBE. Bribing or being bribed in one's dream symbolizes an unsure present and a difficult future.

a. You witness an act of bribery: If the act does not concern your affairs and you do not recognize the persons, it is an open warning to be more serious in your quest for a better life. If you happen to recognize the "briber" or the "bribed" person, it underlines your extremely difficult present situation. If the act concerns you, it means you may get entangled in a lawsuit. If you happen to be bribed and you accept the bribe, it means you are yet undecided and unable to guide your own destiny.

b. You bribe someone: Whether the person accepts your bribe or not, such a dream indicates a very difficult period lying ahead of you. Be more practical.

BRICKLAYER. A bricklayer is a symbol of hard work, perseverance, and hope. A bricklayer also symbolizes ability, good health, and abhorrence of greed and voracity. He also reflects traditional values.

a. You and a bricklayer: Seeing a bricklayer off duty is a sign of hope for the hopeless and those in distress. Seeing him at work is a signal to initiate plans for a constructive life. If he speaks to you, it is a signal to you to eschew greed and voracity. If he gives you something, it means a return to traditional values is imminent in you.

b. You are a bricklayer: Such a dream means good health. It also underscores your happiness and contentment in life. If you appear to be working with other bricklayers, it means you will finally begin to face the challenges in life with a positive outlook. It also means an exit finally from a stagnated period.

BRIDGE. A bridge symbolizes favorable opportunities.

a. You see a bridge: Whether of metal, stone, or concrete, a bridge symbolizes the existence of possibilities within you awaiting full exploitation. It is also a signal to disregard those who appear to discourage you. If the span of the bridge is short, you may attain your aspirations within a short period, while a long bridge, although promising success, will take some time. A broken or a destroyed bridge signifies temporary problems in pursuing your goals.

b. You are crossing a bridge: This is a good sign, assuring that you are on the right path. If you are in a car or appear riding a bicycle, the time period to attain your goals will be short.

BROOM. Several of the "masters" have defined a broom as a presage for a change for the better while some consider it as unfavorable. Several interpretations are listed.

a. You see a broom: This is a signal to begin having hopes in life. It also encourages patience in your expectations.

- A broom assures a sudden change for the better.
- A broom foretells hardships and even a financial loss.

b. You are sweeping: Such a dream means you are nervous due to the problems facing you. If you appear to have finished sweeping a place to your satisfaction, it denotes the end of an unhappy period.

BROTHER. A brother in one's dream, whether younger or older, symbolizes support and courage.

a. You see a brother: If in real life you do not have a brother but in your dream you "see" one, it is a magnificent dream foretelling success to your plans. Since a brother also symbolizes force and energy, you can be assured to flawlessly arrive at your goals. Such a dream also presages good friends who will unwaveringly stand behind you.

b. You see your brother: Any of your brothers signifies an end to a controversial period. It also means good news if you are awaiting an answer to any of your requirements.

BURIAL. Burial in dream symbolizes "burying the past" and the beginning of a new phase in life. It also symbolizes the possibility to solve all outstanding problems.

a. You see a burial: If you know the person to be buried, it means you will very soon have a new beginning in life. If you do not, it means a stranger whom you will soon meet will play an important role in shaping your life. If you happen to participate in a burial ceremony and you are unmarried, a sudden marriage is foretold. If already married, it means a happy married life.

b. You help in the burial: Such a dream foretells good news. If you see any person there whom you recognize, it means help from a family member.

BURNING. The significance of burning in a dream depends on what is being burned and your reaction.

a. You see an unidentified object in flames: Since the object burning in question happens to be lifeless, such as a property, wood, or any other object, it signifies a general loss due to recklessness.

b. You see a human being burning: Burning of a human being ends in ashes. This signifies an end to one particular cycle in life and hence heralds in a new period. Such a dream asks you to try your future with a totally different outlook than you presently have.

c. You see yourself burning: Even if you feel a form of "heat" in your dream arising out of your "burns," it does not signify any form of loss or a grave situation for you. On the contrary, it signifies an imminent change for the better.

BUTCHER. A butcher symbolizes intolerance, anger, revenge, and fraud.

a. You see a butcher: It you just happen to see a butcher, it means you are temperamental and gradually losing your tolerance. If you happen to talk with each other, it means you will have some heated arguments at home that may end in deep misunderstandings. If married, such a dream forebodes quarrels with your spouse.

b. You are a butcher: This is an inauspicious dream, foretelling quarrels that may end in lawsuits. It also means endless litigations and disputes with acquaintances, which may create a revengeful attitude within you. If you happen to be selling meat in the butchery, it denotes a friendly attitude in you, but if you happen to be cutting meat, it suggests a fraudulent behavior within you.

BUTTER. Butter symbolizes easing of difficulties. Usually those on the verge of leaving behind an unfavorable period dream of seeing butter.

a. You see butter: Butter on a plate presages the imminent end to a larger portion of your worries. Seeing it wrapped in paper or cloth speaks of a "ray of hope." At the same time, whether wrapped or open, just being aware that there is butter means there is a friendly compromise on its way for those who are entangled in legal problems. For those separated there are early hopes for a reconciliation.

b. You are eating butter: Such a dream means you have unawaredly entered a new phase in your life, which would essentially be for the better. For those awaiting a decision on inheritance, such a dream presages an unexpected inheritance. Promotion in work and business matters is another significance of this dream.

BUTTON. A button symbolizes a person's character. Depending on the situation of the button and you, an interpretation can be had.

a. You see buttons: If you see buttons lying around, it means that it is about time that you seriously begin thinking about your future. If you appear to be buying buttons, it means you are well aware of the hardships facing you. If one or just a few buttons appear to have come off your shirt, it means your present situation may not ameliorate for some period, but if you dream of having lost all your buttons, it means you must definitely replan your goals as they appear unrealistic, since you are too dreamy. Such a dream also speaks of your illogical approach to life.

b. You are sewing buttons: If you just appear sewing a button, it means you are making efforts to undo the harm that you had yourself inflicted on your situation, while if you dream of having sewn several buttons on your upper or lower garment, it is a good sign promising better days, thanks to your timely awakening.

BUYING. Buying an object or property in one's dream symbolizes a healthy financial situation.

a. You are buying: If you are discussing the possibilities of buying a house and in your conscious life you are in abject poverty, it means things will considerably change to your benefit where you will have the minimum means of subsistence. If you already have a remarkable financial situation and you already own a house, it means further riches through hard and honest work. If you appear to have already purchased a house, it means simply that you will have enough to suit your demands. Buying a small object or an item costing a modest amount means your financial situation will be such that you will be able to lead an average life. Buying any eatable item denotes your strong desire to resist temptations to enter into any unlawful act. Buying a passage (a ticket), whether for a train, bus, or an airplane, presages a new and fruitful beginning in a place far from your present dwelling.

C

CAGE (any cage for birds, animals, and even for holding human beings). A cage in a dream is a symbol of a blockade to one's activities in life. It also means an unpleasant situation where an individual's capabilities will be muffled through conspiracies and jealousies. A cage is a place where one is stifled, strangulated, and even finally destroyed. It has also been described as "a prisoner's dream."

a. You see a cage: A warning of impending miseries unless you drastically change your ways in life. It is also a harbinger of dark days for your entire family if you are the breadwinner. Concentrate on a more positive trade in life.

b. You see yourself in a cage: This embarrassing dream is nothing less than seeing yourself in a prison in a dream. Such a dream signifies a serious warning and even a last-minute signal to "awaken" and reconsider your ways in life. For those involved in legal proceedings, such a dream reminds them that they will be made to atone for their guilt.

CANDLE. A candle is associated with only those with a spiritual leaning. A candle is used by people professing nearly all religions and beliefs. Candles are lighted in a mosque, church, synagogue, temple, and virtually any place of worship. Candles are usually lit before and after prayers are answered by the Almighty. Rarely does an individual with greed, avarice, voracity, and lack of virtue dream of candles.

a. You see a lighted candle or candles: This signifies that your prayers will finally be answered. Your difficulties will be solved and your sadness dispelled. For the helpless, and the homeless, there is a light at the end of the tunnel. If there are several lighted candles, the significance of the dream is strengthened.

b. You light a candle: You have been finally blessed through your prayers. If you had earlier prayed for health, financial, domestic or any other applicable and sane reasons, you have assuredly attained them without being immediately aware. If after lighting the candle you continue to hold the candle in your hand, you are aware of the blessing you have received, but desirous of constantly and endlessly thanking the Creator of the Universe.

c. You see an unlit candle: This is a reminder to repay your debts, at least in words, to your Maker. It also goes to underscore your forgetfulness but not necessarily an ingrate attitude. If you hasten to light the candle, it underscores your spiritual and moral affiliations to life.

d. You buy candles: You will soon receive good news, either of a health recovery of a family member or a friend. Such a dream also means solving of domestic problems to everyone's satisfaction.

CANNON. A cannon, which is a bulky piece of war material, having the potentials for mass destruction, has a good and a bad significance, depending on its situation in general in one's dream.

a. You see a cannon: If you are confronted with several bitter odds in life, a cannon in dream suggests the power to neutralize your foes. But if you are planning to embark on a large-scale investment or any business activity, it reminds you to rethink and replan.

b. You see a cannon being fired: A warning shot to avoid unnecessary risks in your business dealings. It also signals a loss under way for your previous dealings.

c. A cannon is fired at you: This underscores your nervous and timid attitude towards life. Muster courage through meditation.

CANOE.

a. You see a canoe: This means a determined struggle is a must if you desire to translate your plans into reality.

b. You are in a canoe: Being in a canoe tells you that although you have had an encouraging and a correct start, still, you must work your way up. Continue in this spirit. If the water is choppy, the road ahead is very difficult; if the water is calm, the difficulty is lesser. But if you have a person helping you in the canoe, assurances are that the time period in arriving at your goal will be considerably shortened.

CAR. A car or any other vehicle is an auspicious sign, since being on wheels signifies the turning of your wheel of life and going ahead for the better.

a. You see yourself driving a car: Such a dream symbolizes your quest for prosperity and development in life. It also suggests that you are unaidedly and alone bent on changing your destiny for the better.

b. You are being driven in a car: A wonderful dream signifying help and assistance in your endeavors. If you are driving slowly, it foretells a delayed arrival, while driving fast denotes an earlier realization of your goals.

c. You are buying a car: Finally you have decided to utilize your potentials and your possibilities to make efforts in life.

d. You are selling your car: An unfavorable dream underscoring your desires to suddenly discontinue your trade in life. It also foretells a temporary or perhaps a long period of financial instability coupled by domestic problems. Your wheel of life, which may not necessarily stop forever, may however receive a strong setback. Muster courage through concentration and even meditation to fight your lackadaisical behavior.

CARAVAN. A caravan signifies a long but a fruitful journey towards achievement of a particular goal in life. The journey may not be necessarily interpreted in terms of distance and mileage. In fact, it denotes continuity of efforts towards prosperity.

a. You see a caravan: An encouraging sign, which tells you not to be disheartened in your endeavors. It also foresees success in arriving at your goals. If you have any business plans, chances are good for prosperity. If the caravan is moving fast, you will speedily realize your ambitions. A slow-moving caravan, although auspicious, slows the pace of success.

b. You are within a caravan: Time is with you. Patience and honesty will ultimately crown your labors with success. Prosperity and happiness are yours.

CARDS. An inauspicious and an undesired dream. A deck of playing cards or a single card is a harbinger of bad financial standing. Only the debtors, nervous, and fickle-natured usually dream of cards. The reckless and the irresponsible are not excluded.

a. You are playing cards: Whether you win or lose is not the question. Simply playing cards denotes uncertain time ahead of you of which you are perhaps aware and you happen to be the cause of it. For those having such a dream, caution, reticence, and a balanced approach towards everyday life is strongly advocated.

b. You are given a deck of playing cards: Beware of those around you masquerading as your friends. Think for yourself and seek the counsel of a trusted friend or a dependable family member. Refrain from any rash act.

CARPENTER. A carpenter transforms woods and other similar objects into a useful object. Hence, a carpenter in a dream signifies an imminent transformation and a change in an individual's life, essentially for the better.

a. You see a carpenter: A sign that things are on the right track towards prosperity in general.

b. You are a carpenter at work: A good sign that all your efforts aimed at a logical goal will ultimately be realized. You can also expect a total change in your profession and even in your life-style.

c. You argue with a carpenter: An argument with a carpenter often indicates your obstinacy in mending your ways. It also suggests a lack of interest on your part to make the least effort to ameliorate your life, although you have within you all the required possibilities. A friendly conversation, on the other hand, suggests your eagerness to accept expert advice.

CARPET. A carpet (not machine-made but hand-made) is the symbol of fruition of patience, honesty, ability, and hard work. Hence, rarely does a dishonest and a corrupt individual dream of carpets.

a. You see a carpet: It underscores your patience and your abhorrence for greed and vice to arrive at your goals. It also reminds you that honesty and truth finally prevail; however, your life appears to be full of hardships.

b. You see yourself as a carpet weaver: A wonderful dream signifying a "bright light at the end of the tunnel." You will be finally rewarded for your modest, humble, and honest ways in life. Success, even though not on a big scale, appears to be quite near.

c. You are walking on a carpet: The rewards for your labors are on their way. Confidence and respect for you will greatly increase.

d. You are given a carpet as a gift: Receiving a carpet as a gift indicates friends will come to your rescue in the hour of need. It also suggests that you have dependent and honest friends and family members. It may also suggest people's trust in you.

CARRIAGE (horse-drawn carriage). A horse-drawn carriage has both a good and a bad meaning, depending on the situation and its description.

a. You see a carriage with black horses: This is an inauspicious sign of an impending bad development in the family, perhaps death.

b. You see a carriage with white horses: This is an auspicious sign. It signals a celebration, probably due to a promotion, a success in business, recovery from an illness, or even a marriage for those unmarried.

c. You see a carriage without horses: A bad sign, warning you to be more practical and realistic in life. It also means you could have misunderstandings with your wife (if married) or with your friends and family members (if unmarried). Practice restraint and meditate.

CART (a hand cart). A hand cart is a symbol of success through a strenuous path. Since a hand cart is usually pushed or pulled by a single person, it means that there is no sign of outside help or assistance in reaching one's goal. It also symbolizes an individual's arrogance in refusing to accept help from others.

a. You are pulling or pushing a cart: A good sign that you have begun to move in the right direction. If the route appears to be an uphill push or pull, it underscores the temporary difficulties you will face, but if the route is downhill, the path to success appears smoother.

b. You see a cart moving on its own: This is a precursor of a general amelioration in your life. It also means a better financial status and considerable satisfaction in domestic matters.

CASTLE. A castle is a symbol of continuity, power, and grandeur. It is also a symbol of a long life coupled with good health. However, it does not mean excess riches or absolute financial prosperity. The more ancient the castle and well-appearing, the stronger the significance of the dream can be.

a. You see a castle: Seeing a castle in one's dream signifies an improvement in financial matters. Confidence and respect will grow for you. You may also be appointed to some official post. If the castle appears to be far away, the significance is lesser, while if the castle is near, significance increases.

b. You are in a castle: Being in a castle is an indication of holding a responsible socio-political position in the near future. It also signals you to be more serious in order to positively achieve your goals.

CAVE. A cave in a dream denotes a return to primitive behavior and also a total collapse in domestic matters. It is also considered a precursor to unhappiness and even a divorce for those married. In general, it is an inauspicious dream.

a. You see a cave: A warning for those with a quick temper, especially the married. Similarly, it is also a warning for the reckless who spend extravagantly and do not plan for the future.

b. You are in a cave: A further warning of bleak days if you do not immediately mend your ways in life. If there are any living beings in the cave, such as mammals or birds, it signifies that others around you will also suffer due to your faults.

CELEBRATION. Celebration of any religious event in a dream suggests your strong spiritual approach to life. It also underscores your desire to stay away from any worldly sin. Birthday, marriage, or any other celebrations underscore your financial stability.

a. You see a non-religious celebration: Even if it does not concern you, it is a harbinger of good health and financial prosperity. For those in financial difficulty, better days lie ahead; and for the sick, a recovery under way.

b. You celebrate: You are aware of the winds of change that have already affected you for the better. If you continue in the same way, success is yours.

c. You see a religious celebration: A religious ceremony (belonging to any religion) underscores your spiritual approach to life. It also suggests you would soon realize the results of your prayers for an end to misunderstandings within your family.

CEMETERY. A cemetery, although considered an eerie place in reality, is not so in a dream. In a dream, it is considered a place where one particular cycle in life has ended to begin elsewhere in a more flowering manner.

a. You are in a cemetery: This is a precursor of good events to follow very soon. There is every indication that (in case you are embarking on new projects leading to a total change in your life) you will be successful in your business and domestic affairs. Those bearing grudges or animosity against you will ultimately compromise to your satisfaction.

b. You find yourself asleep in a cemetery: This denotes absolute comfort, since you have at least superficially rested your miseries and worries and are ready to change your life as planned.

CERTIFICATE. A certificate in a dream denotes a favorable or an unfavorable sign, depending on the nature of the certificate in question.

a. You are awarded a certificate: Since an awarded certificate usually deals with education or any form of positive achievement, it denotes you will be awarded for your labors and honesty, sooner or later. A sporting-event certificate means continued good health. An educational degree underscores your balance of mind. A property certificate (deed) suggests you will buy a property. A death certificate signifies death, and at the least could mean health problems.

b. You present a certificate to a person: This underscores your helping nature in life. It also means that you will attain such a level in life where you will share the Almighty's grace with His creation.

CHAINING (of a person or animal). Chaining others in one's dream suggests an abnormal behavior. A chain is itself an object of bondage, suffering, hardships, and limitations in one's life. Whether you see it, touch it, or use it on a person or animal in a dream, it signifies your ruthlessness and indifference towards humanity.

a. You are chained up: This suggests you will ultimately be judged for your crimes (if you have committed any) or that your enemies will be successful in their conspiracies to either harm you or to finally destroy you (if you have not acted according to their desires).

b. You chain a person or an animal: Such a dream underscores your brutal and violent behavior and temperament. Such persons must essentially practice meditation, and if possible, immerse themselves in the Book of Scriptures or any other sacred writings.

CHAIR (irrespective of its design). A chair is a significance of authority, negotiation, and even a legal procedure. Depending on your situation and the chair's, an interpretation appears possible.

a. You see a person sitting on a chair lecturing a group seated on the ground: One person speaking to many while seated on a chair foretells a high public position coupled with authority.

b. You see empty chairs around a table: Such a scene foretells an impending legal procedure against you if you fail to amicably compromise or settle your case. If the chairs appear occupied, you could face a trial (not necessarily a criminal case). If you are among the persons sitting around the table, it means you are negotiating a business deal, which would be favorable to you.

CHEATING. Dreaming about cheating or being cheated is considered an undesirable dream. Cheating others suggests you neither depend on others nor do others depend on you. It also underscores your fickle nature, emphasizing your weakness in matters concerning decisions. Cheating in any game related to gambling denotes your awkward approach to life, vis-à-vis simple and daily routines. It also means you are hiding behind a large veil of hypocrisy, risking social distrust. It also denotes a future break in domestic affairs, perhaps a split for those married. Being cheated in a dream does not signify your innocence. Several "masters" are of the opinion that "cheaters are usually cheated ultimately." Hence it could be inferred that such a dream is an unfailing herald of losing ill-gotten wealth or property.

CHEESE. Although cheese is eaten by all, traditionally it is considered as food of the peasants and those within the middle or lower income group. It is also a health food.

a. You are eating cheese: An assurance that you will maintain your standard of living besides a healthy life and a respectable way of living. It also underscores your satisfaction with a simple life and your abhorrence of greed and vice.

b. You are buying cheese: Buying cheese denotes your desire to continue your traditional ways in life, free from all social or financial controversies. It also foretells the fruition of your ambitions and promises a happy married life.

c. You offer cheese to others: Your ambitions are on the verge of fruition. Business and financial matters will prosper. Such a dream calls for thanks to the Creator.

CHESS. Playing chess in a dream is an indication of optimism in the wake of present hardships. Since the game itself is a story of aspiration of victory over a foe, it underlines the dreamer's serious efforts to overcome his difficulties.

a. You are playing chess: An indication of your will to stand up to your problems by tackling them through a positive approach. In case you win, it means that your labors are heading towards fruition. The uphill battle against bitter odds will finally end in your favor. In case you lose, it does not necessarily conclude a defeat in life, but indicates that you have to continue to patiently struggle.

b. You are given a chess set: This means that you will have faithful friends in your struggle to better your lot. It also means that you will choose to arrive at your goals through honesty and fair means.

CHILDREN. It has often been suggested that children are a sign of joy and warmth.

a. You (a woman) see children: For the married, a very happy marriage. For the unmarried, the prospects of a very successful marriage.

b. You (a man) see children: A successful married life together with financial prosperity. If the children appear to be quarreling (which is rarely the case), it warns of impending domestic problems, but which would be temporary and ultimately solved to the satisfaction of all. Children presenting you (a man or a woman) with flowers, fruits, or sweets promise you either a promotion in your job or an unexpected business success.

CHIMNEY. Any chimney emitting smoke is a sign of honesty, hard work, and perseverance. Since smoke from a chimney (a factory's, ship's, house's, workshop's) is related to a productive act, it is a dream usually associated with honest, hard-working, and decent people.

a. You see smoke from any chimney: Smoke from a chimney underscores your honesty, perseverance, and even simplicity in life. It also asks you to uphold and maintain these values in life, which would essentially prove fruitful to you in the long run.

b. You see a smokeless chimney: This dream denotes a lack of a productive activity. A warning not to be tempted or dragged towards any negative acts in order to make a living that could extensively damage your reputation both at home and in the society.

CHURCH. A church is always said to be a place where one seeks nearness with his Creator. There, he usually prays for understanding, peace, happiness, forgiveness of sins, and heavenly guidance, not only for himself as an individual, but for all humanity in general. Any dream pertaining to a church is essentially considered to be one of those dreams that could be definitely called "the best dream." It does not signify financial or any form of worldly gains.

a. You see or approach a church: A wonderful and a desired dream. This suggests you desire to exchange your material gains (if you are very rich) for spiritual gains. It also reflects your intentions to draw yourself away from undesired companions and to follow a decent and honorable trade in life.

b. You are inside a church: A sign that the Creator of the Universe has answered your prayers to be near Him. Calm, tranquillity, and spiritual wealth are yours. A happy domestic life with the required necessities of life is assured.

CIGARETTE. Virtually all the "masters" agreed that a cigar, cigarette, or a pipe that burns tobacco has a negative meaning: the useless burning of mind and body.

a. You see cigarettes: A strong warning that you are wasting your time and your life in general, by pursuing absurd goals. It also indicates a rash behavior and an illogical approach in life.

b. You light a cigarette: This dream dramatizes your nervous behavior. It can also mean a setback in your business or domestic affairs as a result of your own irresponsibility.

c. You are smoking a cigarette: Such a dream underscores your uncomfortable state of affairs, business or otherwise. It may also mean that you have knowingly preferred hopelessness to courage to tackle the bitter odds of life.

d. You are offered a cigarette: A sign to beware of those around you and to refrain from undesired adventurous advice, which could definitely lead to more worries and even to a legal procedure against you.

CINDERS. Cinders in a dream are a reminder that courage coupled with hard work and perseverance finally pays. Usually a dream for the honest.

a. You see hot cinders: A good sign not to despair. The day will come when you will have the chance to prove your worthiness to the society. It is also considered an indicator of hope for the hopeless and a cause of delight for the hapless. Hot cinders also serve as heralder of good news for those ailing.

b. You see cold cinders: Cold cinders in a dream foretell the continuation of the present unhappy period you are experiencing for at least another hundred days. But ultimately, it will end to your satisfaction. Cold cinders are also usually associated with a temporary misunderstanding in one's married life.

CIRCLE. A circle is a symbol of completion and perfection of a cycle in life. A circle in a dream is considered as favorable.

a. You are drawing a circle: A sign of good omen. Drawing a circle in a dream denotes your determination to achieve certain goals in life, however difficult and challenging they may appear.

b. You are seeing a circle that you have just finished drawing: A wonderful dream, signifying that your goals will in general materialize, since you have the possibilities within you. Combining determination that you already have and the existing possibilities, you will achieve positive results.

CITY. A city is a symbol of work, expansion, prosperity, and development.

a. You find yourself in a city: A dream signifying your ambitions will finally materialize. It also means that you can go ahead with your business plans. If you find yourself with some friendly people around you, it indicates you will be helped.

b. You find yourself in a ruined city: A warning of impending financial problems and a possible legal procedure against you. But if you see friendly people, the degree of harm or loss may be greatly lessened.

c. You are leaving a city: Leaving a city means you appear discouraged at your work. Muster courage through meditation.

CLEANING (a place or an object). Cleaning a place or an object signifies getting rid of various obstacles in life. Depending on the place and the object in question, an interpretation could be made.

Places in a house:

a. You are cleaning the rooms: Cleaning rooms is a sign of nearness to achievement of a major business deal. It also means a successful business-related career. If you are being helped, you may have a dependable business partner.

b. You are cleaning the bathroom: A sign of good health. If you are ailing, there is every indication of recovery. It also signifies a balanced and a creative mind.

c. You are cleaning the kitchen: Cleaning and tidying the kitchen signifies the arrival of guests. It also foretells your reunion with old friends.

CLIMBING. Climbing a hill, a steep slope, or any place in a dream signifies your continued perseverance towards perfection; perfection according to your modest possibilities and a will to overcome difficulties.

a. You are climbing a hill or a mountain: This indicates your strong determination to overcome your difficult times in life by undergoing any reasonable hardship. Since climbing a hill or a mountain is sometimes associated with hazards and even risks to life, in a dream it signifies sacrifice and undergoing of limitations to arrive at your goal through honorable means. It also underscores your patience. If you are being helped by being pulled up by another person, your path to attaining your goals will be smoother.

b. You climb a steep slope: The path to arrive at your goals does not appear to be without risks. With care and planning, you will overcome them.

c. You are climbing a tree: Climbing a tree with difficulty or as if in fright signifies your refusal to accept the facts of life, and hence, an escape from it. If you fall while climbing a tree, it is a strong warning to mend your ways in life. If you manage to climb the tree without much effort, it is a sign of success in your goals.

d. You are climbing a ladder: A sign of imminent success in your projects and the full realization of your labors.

CLOCK (a watch or any timepiece).

a. You see a clock or a watch: A timepiece in a dream suggests time is with you. It signifies a major success in business and financial prosperity. If it is a large clock and it appears broken down, it warns you of unpleasant times if you do not move fast enough in life. A broken wristwatch means a temporary setback in your general affairs.

b. You receive a watch as a gift: This means you will be assisted by your family members toward reaching your goals. Coupled with your own hard work and their help, you will achieve your aims. A clock as a gift signifies an easier realization of your goals.

c. You buy a watch: Buying a watch in your dream suggests you are too worried of what is happening around you. It also underscores an impatient behavior.

CLOTHES.

a. You remove your clothes: Deliberately removing your clothes and going around naked underscores your strong desire to remain traditional and simple. It also means you attach great importance to religious and moral values. But if you find yourself naked, it foretells a hard period ahead.

b. You are putting on your clothes: This means you will finally begin to inch your way towards a better period in life. Although the road lies far away, encouraging signs of success will boost your morale to continue the spirit of a positive approach to life.

c. You receive clothes as a gift: A sign indicating a promotion if you are employed, recovery from illness if you are unwell, reconciliation with your family members if misunderstandings exist, and perhaps an unexpected visit from an old acquaintance.

d. You buy clothes: An auspicious dream signifying your determination to start a new life all over again. It also means you will extensively travel in search of finding a new place to settle down.

CLOUDS. Clouds can be interpreted as either good or bad, depending on their color and the situation.

a. You see a clouded sky: If the sky appears heavily clouded and the clouds appear to be of the rainy type, it foretells a breakthrough for the better in your life. If the clouds appear as huge dark patches, it suggests emotional worries and nervousness.

b. You see white clouds: White clouds are considered as a harbinger of good news and an improvement in health, financial situation, and even emotional stability.

c. The clouds partially cover the sun: An indication of hope and faith. A good sign of encouragement, reminding you that your labors will ultimately be rewarded, however, at a modest level.

CLOWN. A clown in a dream symbolizes transiency and even falsehood. As such, it is also said to be a dream of those unsure of themselves, fickle and nervous.

a. You see a clown: This is a warning asking you to be serious and constructive in your approach to life. It also suggests you have a tendency to deviate from your original aims in life.

b. You see yourself as a clown: A dream indicating imminent financial crisis and even a legal procedure arising out of your own irresponsibilities. Pay great attention to your affairs in general and review all your plans for the future.

COAL. Coal in a dream has both a good as well as unfavorable significance. Depending on its situation, an interpretation can be had.

a. You hold a piece of coal in your hand: If the coal is wet, it suggests you are far away from your goals in life. If the coal is dry, it suggests power and a sagacious behavior. A hot coal warns you of your extravagance, which if unchecked could lead you to problems.

b. You see a heap of coal: Whether wet or dry, a heap of coal represents forthcoming worries and endless quarrels within the family. It also suggests an eventual divorce in case a couple is feuding for a considerable period.

COBWEB. A spider's web in a dream has both a good and a bad significance. Depending on the situation, an interpretation can be had.

a. You see a cobweb: If the cobweb is large, intact, and over an opening of any entrance, it suggests you are still a prisoner of your own thoughts through lack of understanding and narrow minded-ness. If a spider is seen either within the cobweb or around it, it means continued problems from those around you who masquerade as friends. But if the cobweb appears torn apart, either with no spider or a dead spider, avenues to a better life appear ahead. It is also an encouraging sign to determinedly act on your own and even search for new friends.

b. You see a cobweb being spun (by a spider): A strong warning much in advance of impending problems, practically in all of your affairs, if you do not act fast to review the repercussions of your present activities.

c. You tear down or destroy a cobweb: A good sign suggesting you have the potentials and the possibilities to be the master of your own destiny. It also means you will relieve yourself from troublesome friends. Business and financial affairs will prosper. Health and domestic affairs will suddenly change for the better.

COFFIN. A coffin symbolizes an end to a particular cycle in life. In fact, it "rings out the old and rings in the new."

a. You see a coffin: An auspicious dream foretelling an early total change in your life-style for the better. It also foretells financial and health recovery. If the coffin appears neat and tidy, it emphasizes the above results, whereas a broken or an untidy coffin suggests delay in arriving at your goals. An untidy coffin also underscores your fickle and nervous nature. An empty coffin means promises by your friends will be unkept.

b. You see yourself lying in a coffin: For the unmarried, a marriage is not far away; for the poor, a financial breakthrough; for the unemployed, employment opportunities. It also suggests an imminent end to misunderstandings among family members and friends.

COFFEE. Presence of coffee in a dream is usually linked with business and financial prosperity.

a. You are drinking coffee: If you are drinking coffee with friends, it means your labors and tireless efforts in the field of business will finally pay off and you will realize the results in less than forty days. If you are drinking coffee alone, it is a sign of encouragement to go ahead with your business deals and perhaps with it, a change in address.

b. You are served coffee: You will embark on a major business affair together with the cooperation of your business associates, which will be fruitful and to your satisfaction. If employed, new proposals are under way, perhaps a promotion. If unemployed, a respectable job suiting your abilities is not far away.

c. You see coffee beans: Coffee beans, though not a good sign, do not necessarily mean something bad. They denote immaturity in thought, body, and spirit, which may lead to temporary setbacks if proper care is not taken.

COIN.

a. **You see coins lying around you:** A symbol of better times. A symbol of progress in your profession and business. If you see a single coin, it denotes the beginning of a period where you will use your imagination and creativity for a meaningful life.

b. **You are given a coin or coins:** This is a warning of impending difficult days due to your own lack of judgment of domestic and financial affairs in life. It also underscores your easy-going and irresponsible approach to basic matters of life. A cautious philosophy coupled with an expert's counsel would help.

COLD (feeling cold in a dream).

a. **You feel cold:** Feeling cold in one's dream suggests discomfort in your thoughts arising out of your own untoward acts vis-à-vis your family members, friends, and the society in general. It underscores a faint form of "harmless" hypocrisy. It also suggests you are continuously dodging realism and clinging to unrealistic values, although you do not mean harm to others.

b. **Your limbs are cold:** If you feel cold either in the hands or feet, it suggests your nervousness and anxiety has reached intolerable heights. Meditation appears to be a good means of calming down.

COLORS. Colors underscore and reflect the positive and negative forces and also the feelings within a human being. Wherever deemed necessary a word of admonishment accompanies the interpretations. Colors could be "seen" on a house, any monument, trees, birds, or any vehicle. A patch of any color elsewhere, such as on clothes or an animal, may also be considered.

Black: This color symbolizes absolute recklessness and the disregard to life by taking risks whose consequences you do not care to

51

understand. Such a color in dream asks you to be rational, reasonable, and wise.

Blue (dark shade): Dark blue reflects a mysterious and an undependable character. If you see it on any individual whom you recognize, it warns you to beware of him. If you do not know that person, it is a general warning. On a woman it warns of violence. On any type of building or wall, it asks you to practice restraint on your fiery temper. On any vehicle, a bird, or any moving object, it forebodes a violent death due to revenge. If someone appears to paint this color on you, a former friend will deceive you. Be more realistic and responsible.

Blue (light shade): Light blue reflects the vast expanse of space, the sky, and the infinite possibilities for one's spiritual development. This color also underscores the high degree of importance you attach to moral values. If a priest, a nun, or a theologian and you see this color, it means you will continue to pursue your goals to the required standard that would be to your satisfaction.

Brown (dark shade): Dark brown reflects irrelevance, indecision, and inability to face the least uneasiness in life. A dream for the lazy and lethargic. This color is rarely seen by those who are realistic and practical. This color in a dream reminds the dreamer that in case anything concrete is to be attained immediate steps have to be taken and that the time for the initiation of action is not tomorrow but now. Develop a will to do things.

Brown (light shade): This color, unlike the dark shade, reminds one of the potential within one to begin in earnest the quest for his goals. At this juncture, it is necessary to remind that since the dreamer's goals appear lawful and even modest, this color is a signal to "go ahead," since the plans would materialize. Rarely do those indulging in vice or unlawful acts dream this color. Go ahead with courage, since destiny is with you.

Green (any shade): This color if seen by a woman has no significance. This color, if seen by a man, reflects a woman's or a wife's evil intentions. It underscores the continued fear you have from her of either being blackmailed, threatened, or tormented. Here, logic and common sense dictate that you use your power of understanding and comprehension. If in the conscious state the woman in question (only if you recognize her in your dream) is fair, honest, and friendly, such a color only serves to awaken from the false illusions you have of her, but if in the conscious state you suspect her of being evil, sagacity and a quick presence of mind are advocated. If you do not have a woman or a wife and you dream so, then it is a warning not to have illusions of others, since such a behavior will mentally ruin you.

Orange: Just as the color "light blue," the color orange or even saffron is a dream for those immersed in the world of spiritualism and meditation. For those who appear weakened or discouraged from their quest for spiritual gains, this color reminds them that their efforts will not be in vain. If you find yourself dressed in orange or saffron, it underscores your desire to shun materialism for spiritualism.

Red: This color reflects fiery temper, continued anger at injustice, and the urge to strike back at antagonizers. Hence, any person with such a character who sees such a color is strongly urged to practice restraint, since the results would be tragic. Such a color in a dream in fact reminds the dreamer of the wisdom of retaliating or taking revenge. Meditation and prayers are advised.

White: The significance of this color in a dream depends on who sees it. A person of normal character can expect a continued period of tranquillity. Hence, this color reflects his calm and friendly temperament while if seen by a revengeful person, it underscores his violent means in life and hence betokens a tragic ending for him. But since he has seen this color in his dream, it is a strict warning of the impending developments and as such, his early response to deal with his situation will greatly help him overcome any future tragedy. Meditation, reading the scriptures, and a regular visit to any place of worship will greatly heal the emotional outbursts.

Yellow: This color reflects inability in general due to nervousness, continued fatigue due to neglect of health, and the absence of any urge to follow a positive goal in life. The dreamer is admonished to create within himself confidence, so that the urge to achieve a goal, however modest, will at least begin.

COMET. The sighting of a comet is usually associated with a major event affecting the earth. It is also accepted that the events will not be too favorable, which are usually in the form of earthquakes, volcanic eruptions, floods, and other calamities.

a. You (a man) see a comet: A harbinger of an unfavorable event. Perhaps a feud in the family or a heated argument, even leading to separation or divorce (if you are married), an undesired development in your place of work leading to an unpleasant result, a sudden loss in business or other major upsets at family level.

b. You (a woman) see a comet: If you see a comet streaking towards the skies, and if you are an expecting mother, take great pains to control your temper. It may foretell unexpected unhappiness, perhaps a quarrel with your in-laws or a still-born child.

COOKING. Cooking in a dream is a good sign. Cooking symbolizes nourishment, health, and a modest life.

a. You are cooking for yourself and others: Cooking for others underscores your selfless character and reflects your desires of helping and feeding others. If cooking for yourself alone, it means temporary loneliness.

b. You see someone cooking: This means had it not been for examples set by your friends, you would have drowned yourself in undesired problems due to your uncontrolled temperament. It also suggests a successful conclusion to your simple desires in life, which would be realized only through help from family members.

CORPSE. A corpse in a dream symbolizes impending difficulties in several spheres of your life.

a. You see a corpse: Domestic misunderstandings, a sudden breakage in friendship, an impending quarrel, often ending in violence, and a worsening of illness are usually associated with a corpse in a dream.

b. You see a woman's dead body: A woman's dead body denotes either an illness, hardship, or even death for a female family member. For married men, it could mean an unpleasant separation or divorce.

c. You see a man's dead body: Several "masters" claim the dead person's corpse is in reality the reflections of your own being fallen in such a situation, due to your own irresponsibilities. Hence, a strong warning to mend your ways.

COUNTRYSIDE. A beautiful countryside in a dream is often attributed to positive results of your labors and hard and honest work.

a. You find yourself in a countryside: If green and beautiful, it foretells your success in business, employment, and even domestic affairs. If barren, it indicates a defeat and even retreat from life.

b. You are leaving a countryside: If you are leaving a beautiful countryside, it presages a sudden setback in business, which could be overcome through a sagacious approach. If you are leaving a barren and a desolate countryside, it is a harbinger of good news. It could also mean a fresh start in life for the better.

COURT (a court of law). A court of law in a dream symbolizes dishonesty within a person. A court with a friendly atmosphere symbolizes financial gains through inheritance.

a. You appear confronted in a court: This specifically indicates some dishonesty within you for which you will be answerable sooner or later.

b. You have a pleasant conversation in a court: This foretells you will be named as an inheritor of a property from a source you least expected.

c. You are ordered to present yourself in a court: Such a dream is a precursor of a legal proceeding against you. If you appear arrested and being led to a court, it means imprisonment or a fine. If you go voluntarily, it suggests an end to the case through a friendly compromise.

COURTYARD.

a. You are in a courtyard: This reflects your satisfaction at your achievements, however modest they are. It also means you have undergone considerable stress for a little reward. Being in a courtyard (for those divorced or separated) signifies a reconciliation in the near future.

b. You see yourself with friends in a courtyard: This suggests a happy ending to family disputes. If food and refreshment are also served, it means you have overcome a larger part of your difficulties.

c. You see workers working in a courtyard: A good dream suggesting your friends will sincerely do whatever is possible in their capacity to help you. An assurance that you will not be left alone.

CRADLE.

a. You see an empty cradle: A warning to beware of unrealistic plans and to begin with something more practical. It is also a warning of future problems arising from your empty promises to yourself.

b. You see a cradle with a baby: A good sign, promising possibilities to get a start in life. It also suggests friends and family members will come to your help in unhappy times. A sleeping baby in a cradle is a sign of calm and tranquillity within you while a cradle with a crying baby denotes difficulties in arriving at your goals.

CRIME. Crime in dream symbolizes an uncomfortable period. Just as it is a negative act in real life, crime in dream means a person is drowned in wicked thoughts and may enact it in real life.

a. You commit a crime: In a dream, any act legally considered unlawful and against all norms of decency underscores your desire in real life to commit such an act. It may suggest you have already begun to nurture evil thoughts and may soon enact them. Since there is no excuse to commit any crime, even for the sake of honor or conscience, a crime in a dream under any pretext reflects your intention in daily life. Meditation and regular visit to a place of worship may relieve you of such thoughts.

b. You see others committing a crime: A strong warning of an impending legal procedure against you if you go ahead with the criminal intentions you have already nurtured.

CROSS. A cross, in whatever design and material, is a symbol of spiritual calm and blessing. It also signifies a simple and an uneventful social life.

a. You see a cross: If the cross is unusually large, it is a sign for you to discontinue your greedy and voracious life-style. If it is of a normal size meant to be worn around the neck, it reminds you of the spiritual values of life.

b. You receive a cross as a gift: If it is given by a religious figure, it denotes your satisfaction in life, since it foretells your desire to exchange "spiritual wealth" for the material wealth that you already have. A cross as a gift also means your family will have a simple and a meaningful life and away from social tie-ups.

CROWN. A crown in a dream symbolizes prestige, position, and respect.

a. You see a crown: Seeing a crown in one's dream signifies a promotion in job or a breakthrough in business affairs. A crown also foretells a successful marriage for the unmarried and for those married a happy life.

b. You crown yourself: A dream suggesting your dishonest behavior. It also emphasizes your egoistic approach to life and underlines your uncompromising nature.

c. Others crown you: A good sign, which will increase people's confidence in you. You may also be appointed to a responsible position, if employed. It may also presage a victory in being elected for public duty.

CRUTCHES.

a. You are walking with crutches: This foretells a long and a tiring journey towards achieving your goals. Since crutches are a means of assisting you to walk, it also denotes an unexpected help, but just the same, the goal appears quite far.

b. You receive a pair of crutches: A good dream signifying an end to your petty problems. It also means better times relating to finance and business affairs.

CRY. Crying symbolizes both favorable as well as unfavorable significances, depending on who is crying.

a. You cry with sadness in your dream: A good omen, suggesting an end to domestic worries. If married and faced with misunderstandings from your partner, you can expect a satisfying compromise. If due to the intensity of your own crying you wake up, this suggests financial prosperity and even success in love.

b. You see an old person crying: If it is an old man, it foretells a sudden death in the family. If an old woman is crying, it suggests breakup of a marriage.

c. You see a crying child: A crying child suggests a happy married life. For the unmarried, a sudden and an unexpected marriage.

CUP. A cup in a dream has several significances. Depending on its situation, an interpretation can be had.

a. You see a cup: If the cup is beautiful and full, it denotes you are in the prime period of your life. It also means that you will enjoy peaceful and happy moments for a long period. If the cup is beautiful but empty, it denotes an artificial life coupled with internal worries. If the cup is broken and empty, it suggests your friends will leave you in the hour of need. This warns you to quit depending on others.

b. You break a teacup: This warns of impending financial losses. It also suggests your temperament always gets the better of you. Practice restraint and calm.

c. You are offered a cup with tea or any other warm liquid: A wonderful dream signifying sudden good news, which will fully change your life for the better.

CURTAIN.

a. You see a curtain: A large curtain dividing two rooms is often associated with secrecy. Such a dream suggests one or more of your family members are hiding something from you.

b. You raise or open the curtains: This suggests you will ultimately triumph over unjustified criticism leveled against you by those pretending to be your friends. It also means the completion of a business deal or any other personal project. Raising or opening curtains can also mean exposing those responsible for your unhappiness.

CUT. A mistakenly self-inflicted cut, which results in flow of blood, has little or no significance. But if someone else cuts you accidentally, it could mean that you are very careless. So are your associates. But if there is a lot of blood flowing from the cut, the dream could be considered as organic and, hence, has no value in terms of interpretation.

a. You are cut intentionally: Beware of those claiming to be your friends. It also suggests a conspiracy against you in love matters by those whom you consider "friends."

b. You intentionally cut somebody: You are getting rash and nervous due to negligible matters. This also means you are heading for some domestic misunderstandings.

D

DAGGER. A dagger symbolizes deceit and ungratefulness. It also signifies unknown enemies, some even masquerading as friends.

a. You see a dagger: If seen to be lying on a table or any other raised surface, it is a warning to be on your guard and to stop having "confidence" in friends or those around you. If seen lying on the floor, it means you have already made several enemies and it is time to disassociate yourself from them. If seen in the hands of a person who does not threaten you, it means you must refrain from entering into any form of argument with people. If the dagger appears sheathed and appears to be lying in any place, the negative effects of the dream will be less.

b. You have a dagger in your hand: If you appear to threaten or intend harm to anyone, such a dream underscores your temperament and easily agitated behavior. Practice calm and restraint through meditation.

c. You are threatened with a dagger: If by someone you know, it means your progress will be hindered through your own faults. If you do not recognize the person threatening you, it means a short difficult period to be followed by a marked amelioration.

DANCING. Dancing symbolizes joy and good news.

a. You are dancing: Dancing in one's dream with a partner signifies the arrival of beneficial news, while dancing alone has two significances: either a complete satisfaction with your own performance in life or a help or gift is already on the way that will add to your happiness.

b. You see people dancing: If you appear to be watching others dance, it means there is every reason for a modest celebration since after long periods of waiting, you will finally have justice for your labors.

c. You are invited to a dancing party: This suggests good news from your family members. It may also mean a new employment proposal.

DANGER. Danger symbolizes uneasiness and anxiety within.

a. You see yourself in danger: If you see yourself in danger of being killed, it means that your acute anxiety over a certain development appears to have taken over all your energies. If you harbor dislike for any individual and you see him as posing a danger to your life, it means that although there is no danger from his side, you continue to think of that particular person as a source of danger. If that person tells you that he will ultimately "finish" you or take revenge on you, it means that through a better comprehension of your surroundings you can gain more calm and solace. If you appear falling from a height, it suggests nervousness still persists within you, perhaps for no logical reason. If you appear in danger of suffocation, it denotes petty family feuds that require sorting out. If you appear in danger of drowning, it foretells miseries and mental worries as a result of your past and present activities that need mending.

b. You see danger pass by you: A good sign, indicating moral and physical recovery. If you safely pass away from any source of danger in general, it means you will gradually overcome your hardships through perseverance and concerted efforts.

DARKNESS. Darkness in a dream is usually attributed to one's "ups and downs" in life and its results. Depending on the situation, several other interpretations can be had.

a. You suddenly find yourself in absolute darkness: Such a dream means you appear to have been kept unaware of events confronting you either through conspiracies and jealousies or that you yourself have not been careful enough to foresee the results of your acts. Only a determined approach to your affairs could help extricate you.

b. You walk from sunlight into darkness: This means that you are losing your courage at the first sight of a simple challenge in life. It is also a sign of self-created unhappiness which will last until you are able to muster enough courage to deal with the situation. As such, it reflects the lackadaisical spirit within you.

c. You walk from the darkness (an underground cave, tunnel, or hole) into the sunlight: An encouraging dream, suggesting your determination to lead a normal life through hard work. It also means a further prosperity in life.

DAUGHTER. A daughter in a dream is a sign of joy. It also means an end to domestic problems. But at certain times, depending on the daughter's behavior and situation, it can be an unfavorable dream.

a. You see your daughter: If your daughter appears in a friendly manner and happy, it is a favorable sign in general for the family. If she appears to be either unhappy or complaining, it means there are several problems to be straightened out very soon. If she appears overgrown or bitterly attacks her husband or future husband (if a grown daughter), it means there will be major setbacks in the family. But if she is small and chides you or your spouse (any of her parents), it means you have not been doing your duties well and as such could face an embarrassing situation within a fortnight. If the daughter is unmarried but appears pregnant, it is a sign of deep conflict within the family, but if she is married and you dream of her as being pregnant, it is a sign of calm days. If your daughter appears to attack you either physically or verbally, it is a sure sign of her ingrate character. If she introduces someone to you as her future spouse, it is a good sign of financial prosperity. But if you have such a dream more than once and if the character introduced happens to be another person, it is a direct prophecy that your daughter will have bitter days ahead of her. To see your daughter singing, dancing, writing, weaving, walking, or swimming presages a sudden development within the household, often for the better. To see your daughter sick or crying forebodes a quarrel within the family.

DEAFNESS. Being deaf in a dream symbolizes continued irresponsibility and laziness.

a. You are deaf: Being deaf in a dream underscores your indifference to society and things to do with your daily life. If you continue this trend, you will only accumulate further problems, which will be difficult to solve. Be more practical and realistic.

b. You speak to a person whom you find to be deaf: Take great care to avoid any rash decision, such as selecting a partner in life, a business partner, a friend, and even a profession.

DEATH. Death in a dream has the opposite meaning. It means a long and a healthy life coupled with prosperity. It also means a new life with new friends.

a. You dream of your own death: Such a dream means that the several setbacks in your life have ultimately made you feel that now it is the time for you to get moving towards a new horizon in life. Since the urge within you has extensively increased and you appear ready to meet the challenge, seeing your own death is in fact a signal that things will go along as planned. Muster enough courage and confidence through meditation.

b. You witness the death of others: If you know the dead person and if he is sick, he will recover if his illness is not terminal or dangerous. If that particular person is in misery or poverty, he will recover his financial status and if you do not recognize the person, it means that through the intervention of either an acquaintance or even a family member, your general situation will greatly ameliorate. A dead body lying on the ground means imminent help from quarters you least expected while a body floating on water promises a sudden breakthrough for the better.

DECEPTION. Deceiving any person or being deceived in a dream symbolizes the urgent need to beware of one and all.

a. You and deception: If you doubt your wife in the conscious state and you dream of being frightened of her deceptive ways, it is a strong warning to take great care while dealing with her. If you doubt your husband and you dream of his deception, it means you (the wife) are not being serious enough to tackle the difficulties of life. But if you dream of deceiving someone in your dream, it means that you are still harboring hatred for a particular person or more, which will eventually have great strains on your mental faculty. If someone teaches you to deceive someone and if you happen to know that person, it is a strong warning to keep away from that person, but if you do not recognize that person, it means that you are beginning to indulge in untoward methods in life that could greatly hinder your progress in life and that could also smear your name in the society. Practice calm and contentment through prayers and meditation.

DEMOLISHING. Since the act of demolition is intentional and for reasons, it depends on what object or place is being demolished in order to have an interpretation.

a. You see a house being demolished: If it is your own house and it is being demolished on your instructions, it suggests a new and a more worthy life coupled with spiritual gains. But if the house appears to be demolished against your desire, it means that due to your own carelessness in life you will be confronted by losses leading to untold unhappiness. If a building is being demolished, it suggests a general hardship.

b. You demolish a snake's pit: A good sign that you have finally escaped from the clutches of evil acquaintances. It also means that you have decided to depart from the sinful life that you have led so far. It may also mean your sudden awakening to approach the Almighty.

c. You demolish a bird's nest: Such a dream underlines your unforgiving nature. Practice tolerance and compassion through reading the holy Scriptures.

d. You see a bridge being demolished: If near it means you have done considerable damage to your prestige through unlawful deeds. If far it is a warning to immediately change your ways in life, since there is still some chance for you to change. If far, such a dream serves as a warning to refrain from any negative act.

DESERT. Desert symbolizes bitterness, hardships, and sadness coupled with loneliness. As such a desert in a dream is considered chiefly as unfavorable except for a few instances.

a. You and a desert: If you appear suddenly in the midst of a desert, it means that your wife, if you are married, will be the chief source of your mental tortures and, if you are unmarried, it means your future wife will not be as good as she may claim to be. Such a dream admonishes great care in choosing your wife. If you appear to see some greenery or a settlement in the distance or near, it means that the danger from the woman will itself recede, thanks to your reticent ways in life. If in the desert you come across your spouse, it means you will have a financial loss. If you see your friends in the desert, it is a sure sign of consolation. If you appear tired, hungry, thirsty, naked or sitting down in the midst of a desert, it means that you are on the verge of giving up all hopes, but there is no need to worry, since the desert with its sands also symbolizes temporary hardship and hence your determination coupled by genuine efforts will set your wheels of life and living once more into motion. If you appear to be eating something in a desert, it means your own labors will ultimately help you and warns you not to depend on false promises.

DESK. A desk has both a good as well as a bad significance, which depends on your situation vis-à-vis the desk.

a. You are sitting idly behind a desk: Such a dream warns of an impending financial loss and even bankruptcy if proper care is not taken.

b. You see a desk: A large desk with documents, papers, or books signifies that times will change for the better with a little effort. If the table appears empty, it denotes a period marked by unemployment and domestic problems.

c. You are working behind a desk: Such a dream underscores your determination to better your lot through patience. But beware of any haphazard move and refrain from entering into any new business ventures until you are assured that your past efforts bear fruits. If you appear sleeping on the desk, it reflects your deep interest to show your capacity to do things.

d. You buy a desk: Buying a desk means that you are contemplating the right thing at the right time, while disposing of, selling, breaking, or breaking up a table reflects the deep depressive mood within you.

DESTRUCTION (of a place, property, surrounding). Finding yourself amidst a destroyed region is usually done without justification but for negative purposes, as the word itself implies. Destruction of a place has several significances, favorable as well as otherwise, but strictly depends on the place destroyed.

a. You see a place of worship destroyed: Whether a mosque, a church, a synagogue, a temple, or other place of worship, if any one of these places appears destroyed, in ruins, or set on fire, it forebodes a tense period laced with anger, violence, arguments, and even legal problems. In short, such a dream reflects the deep anger within you for not meeting the required success you had expected. If you see workers or persons trying to restore the destroyed place, it means a last-minute effort coupled with help would greatly ease your problems. Control your emotions through continued prayers and meditation.

b. You see a center of vice or corruption destroyed: Such a dream presages a happy ending to your griefs and sorrows. It also means that within the next forty days you will receive the fruits of your labors and honesty.

c. You see a center of education destroyed: Any center of education lying in ruins or destroyed means the end of your educational career through your own faults.

d. You see a recreational center destroyed: Such a dream forebodes illness due to carelessness. Take great care of your most dear possession: your health.

e. You see other places destroyed: Seeing your own house destroyed or lying in ruins suggests a general loss due to your lack of ability to manage your affairs. Seeing unidentified houses in ruins denotes an unhealthy atmosphere in your place of work. Seeing a prison destroyed or lying in ruins denotes the end of hardships. It also means a favorable end to any legal problems. Seeing a hospital in ruins or being pulled down denotes ill health due to misuse of one's body either by alcohol, drugs, or other unhealthy agents, while a village in ruins means the end of an ominous cycle in life.

DEVIL. Since a devil has been conceived as having a certain form, any resemblance to this evil being is considered a devil. A devil nevertheless symbolizes unfavorable temptations.

a. You see a devil: If the devil appears to be near you, it foretells a strong temptation within you to indulge in unlawful acts that will eventually bring you unbearable unhappiness. If the devil and you exchange any friendly conversation, it denotes impending danger either through accident, drowning, or violence. Seeing a devil in one's dream necessitates prayers and reading of the Scriptures.

b. You confront a devil: Either verbally or physically or even a weak attempt to confront his presence is considered a good omen, since it means that you will be able to tactfully overcome your problems.

DIAMOND. Diamonds in a dream symbolize false illusions, illness, and loss.

a. You see diamonds: A strong warning to do away with false illusions and to approach life more realistically. If you find yourself with a diamond either around your neck or on a ring or you have it in your hands, it forebodes illness or a violent confrontation with a family member.

b. You find a diamond: Such a dream means that you are heading for a business loss. Take great care to plan all your business activities.

c. You receive diamonds: If you (a woman) get one as a gift from a person other than your husband, it foretells a severe misunderstanding with your husband, which could lead to a very ugly situation. Choose well the words you intend to use at home. If you (a man) receive a diamond from your wife, it is a sure sign that your wife is not only dishonorable but that she is outrightly a thief, but if you are presented one by either your son or daughter, it is a good sign promising prospects in your financial affairs.

DIGGING. Digging in one's dream has a good as well as a bad significance. Depending on what is being dug, an interpretation can be had.

a. You are digging a grave: This is a good sign, promising a new beginning in life, but if you see others digging a grave, it is a signal to accept the wise advice of friends and family members.

b. You are digging for water: An unfavorable dream for those in business foretelling financial loss. For those not in business, it could mean alienation from family members.

c. You are digging to plant a tree: A good dream underscoring your determination to prosper through honest means. It also underscores your religious inclinations.

d. You are digging for precious metals: Such a dream means that you are still living in a world of illusions. Be more practical.

e. You see others digging: If you see others digging for whatever purpose and if there is at least a house or residence nearby, it is a sign of general amelioration in life.

DIRT. Dirt of any type symbolizes a general setback. As such, it is considered unfavorable in one's dream.

a. Your body is dirty: Such a dream reminds you to be more careful, prudent, and active. Such a dream also symbolizes your carefree style of life. If you see dirt on your spouse's body, it means she has not been living to the required standard or that she has been deceiving you till today.

b. Your clothes are dirty: If your clothes alone appear dirty, it means that you have not been making the required efforts in life but leaving everything to the fate of destiny. But if both your clothes as well as your body appear dirty, it could signal a long period of illness, often ending in tragedy. If you see any of your children in such a situation, it means that you have not been a responsible person.

DIVORCE. The significance of a divorce in a dream depends on who dreams of seeking or getting one and has significance only for those married.

a. You (a man) speak or plan to divorce your wife: Such a dream underscores your easily agitated behavior, which will earn you a long period of unhappiness. If in the conscious state you have planned such a thing and you regularly dream about seeking a divorce, it means that you have jumped to a wrong conclusion. Practice calm and meditation, which could greatly relieve the stress within you. If you happen to directly seek a divorce with your wife in your dream and if she consents, it means that your wife is honorable and if she refuses and argues or appears violent, it means she is evil within.

b. You (a woman) speak or plan to divorce your husband: Whether you appear to have been divorced or you appear to seek one, such a dream suggests stability and an exceptionally good relation with your husband. It may also include a temporary souring of relations.

DOCTOR. Since a doctor is a symbol of treatment and cure, his presence is considered a harbinger of good health and prosperity.

a. You see one or more doctors: One or more doctors at a distance or nearby symbolize good friends who will be pleased to assist you in the hour of need.

b. You meet or speak with a doctor: If sick or ailing, such a dream means that you are on the way to recovery if the illness is minor.

c. A doctor visits you: A harbinger of prosperity and financial gains, although modest. If the doctor praises you, it means that things will turn to your favor.

DOLL. Dolls symbolize falsehood and deceit.

a. You see a doll: If you see any aged person with a doll, it means that you must not trust anyone without being sure of their motives. If you see dolls in a room, it means there are conspiracies going around against you. If you see yourself with a doll, it means that you are living in a fool's paradise.

b. You buy a doll: Buying a doll means you will soon make friends who will turn out to be not only useless but also dangerous. If you see a doll with your wife or if she happens to present one to you, it is a sure sign of deceit from her, which you will greatly regret unless you move fast enough to thwart any of her evil plans.

c. You burn, throw away, or destroy a doll: Such a dream signifies your determination to finally "get up" from your dreamy ways and be serious and realistic.

DOOR. A door in a dream symbolizes opportunities for success and a better life filled with modest happiness.

a. You see a door: If the door appears open, it suggests unlimited opportunities for you to try your luck, whether in business, employment, or education. If the door appears partially closed, it means you have to make some efforts to create the possibilities within you to arrive at your goals. If the door appears closed, there would be struggles involved although you would be ultimately successful.

b. You see an old or a broken door: An old door means you have been indifferent to the several chances you had in life whereas a broken door signals the virtual end of good chances in life.

c. You install a door: A wonderful dream signifying a good period within the next forty days. But it must be borne in mind that you must continue your quest to reach your goals.

DOORBELL. A doorbell or even its sound symbolizes joy and happiness.

a. You see or hear a doorbell: Just seeing or hearing a doorbell signifies either a visit from a much-liked family member, a good friend, or, plainly speaking, very good news. But if you appear to press the doorbell of any house (other than your own), it means that

70

very soon you will meet a person whose presence will greatly alter your life-style.

DRINKING. Drinking in one's dream has both a favorable as well as an unfavorable significance, depending on what is being drunk.

a. You are drinking water: If you appear to be drinking potable water, it is a sign of continued good health. If you are ill with minor ailments, such a dream presages a quick recovery. Drinking muddy or unclean water signifies an impending illness or domestic problems. But if you appear to be drinking water from a fountain and regardless of the quality of the water, it means financial prosperity and domestic satisfaction. If your spouse offers you water, it is a sign of her good will and if your children offer you, it means you will have faithful children.

b. You are drinking wine or other intoxicating drinks: If you appear to be drinking wine with friends, it means you will soon arrive at your modest goals, but if you appear to be drinking alone, it forebodes some loss and domestic problems whose chief cause will be your wife. If unmarried, beware of your lover. If you appear to be drinking strong alcoholic drinks, whether in the company of friends or alone, it means that you must move fast to replan your activities before you face a devastating period.

DRIVING. Driving, depending on how you appear to drive, symbolizes your emotions.

a. You are driving a vehicle: If you appear to be well in control of the vehicle, it means you are at the helm of your destiny and need no outside interference. If at the same time you appear to be driving slowly, it means that your progress will be to your liking, but if you appear to be speeding, it means a very hasty attempt at your goals with a questionable result.

b. You are being driven: If you are being driven around in a car, it means that you will receive some assistance that will greatly enhance your situation. But if you are being driven forcefully or to an unknown destination or against your will, which may even amount to you being abducted, it means great mental worries at your place of work, domestic problems, and quarrels with your spouse, often ending in an ugly situation. If you had recently some misunderstandings with an acquaintance or even with your spouse, calm and restraint are advocated.

DROWNING. Drowning in one's dream is an unfavorable dream. It presages untold hardships.

a. You dream you are suddenly on the verge of drowning: Such a dream warns you that your past and present activities will be responsible for submerging you in untold miseries. If a gambler, quit gambling; if an alcohol abuser, quit drinking; and if indulging in any sort of vice or unlawful acts, quit doing so. If you (a woman) are habituated to argue or quarrel with your husband and you see such a dream, it means that you will end by disgracing yourself and if you (a man) dream of drowning and if you have bickerings with your wife, you must understand that either you must be sagacious enough to evade her words or wisely confront her falsity. If you dream that you are being drowned by any family member, it is a direct sign of their ingrate behavior. If any of your children or spouse happens to be drowning you, such a dream speaks of an uncertain life with them.

DRUGS (narcotics). Since drugs in any form are considered agents that gradually and progressively destroy a human being's mind and body, any sign of abusing drugs in a dream is considered a harbinger of mental torture, physical destruction, and financial misery leading to poverty and other tragedies. In dreams too their significance is ominous.

a. You see drugs or narcotics: Just seeing drugs lying anywhere in a dream is a direct warning to mend your ways immediately. If you are a drug abuser and you see them, such a dream forebodes terrible consequences if you continue to use them. If someone offers drugs to you and if you accept them, it means that you are unaware of your general situation that would not be too favorable. But if you refuse them, there is every chance that you will arrive at your modest goals in life with your own efforts.

b. You see people using drugs: Seeing people using drugs means that you are too perplexed as to what should be your next move.

DUMBNESS. Dumbness in one's dream signifies weakness to confront your tormenters. Depending on your situation, other interpretations can be had.

a. You are dumb: If you have recently had any confrontation with someone (this includes your family members, spouse, or an acquaintance) and you feel wronged and at the same time unable to raise your voice against that person in question and if you feel or appear dumb in your dream, it means that although you are weak, law and justice will ultimately side with you. If you have recently indulged in any wrongdoing or you are awaiting the result of a legal proceeding where you know that you are not innocent, such a dream forebodes a defeat in the wake of justice. Under such circumstances such a dream also means that it would be futile to defend your cause since you have caused enough damage to your spiritual and moral faculties. If a woman finds her husband dumb in her dream, it means she is up to some fraud against her husband, her sister, and even against her own parents.

b. You see a dumb person: If you recognize that person and if that person is dumb in the conscious state, it means that it is time to have courage to face the world, and if you do not recognize that person, it means that you will be discouraged through jealousies. Quarreling with a dumb person in one's dream signifies your inability to comprehend the basic facts of life. If you see one or more dumb persons quarreling with each other, it speaks of impending financial losses due to your extravagant ways.

DUNG. Dung symbolizes a total amelioration in one's life. As such, it is considered a favorable dream.

a. You see dung around you: A good sign foretelling a general change for the better. If in business, you can expect things to go smoothly and if employed, you can expect a promotion. If you are poverty-stricken, your situation will change much to your surprise.

If ill, a partial recovery is presaged. If you have a legal case pending against you and you are sure that you are innocent, a speedy decision in your favor is inevitable within the next forty days.

b. You utilize dung or spray it on the field: An indication that you will witness the fruition of your labors very soon. Such a dream also underscores your motto to succeed only through hard and honest work.

c. Dung is thrown at you: If someone throws dung at you, it is an unmistakable sign of receiving a costly gift very soon and if you fall in a heap of dung, it denotes property through inheritance.

DWARF. A dwarf in a dream foretells a change in your life either for the better or for the worse, depending on your situation in the dream.

a. You dream you are a dwarf: If you dream you have become a dwarf, it denotes a demotion in your general status in society. If employed, any promotion or even stability is out of the question. If a businessman, profits will not be realized as expected. If a gambler, you will experience regrets. In general seeing yourself as a dwarf is an ominous omen. Take great care and practice caution. If you are a dwarf in the conscious state and dream of having a normal build, such a dream presages prosperity and happiness.

b. You see dwarfs around you: A favorable dream foretelling a sudden and a complete change in your life. If unmarried, it could mean a successful matrimonial alliance that could bring you immense happiness. If you appear to attack a dwarf in your dream and if he bleeds or even falls on the ground, it forebodes a death in the family.

DYING (see also DEATH). Seeing a person on the verge of death or seeing yourself dying serves as a warning to take great care of your health and your life as well.

a. You see someone dying: If one sees such a dream, it foretells an accident due to negligence, which could prove dangerous to life. If you see the dying person writing a letter or anything else, it means a sudden change in your life for the better. If someone tells you that such and such a person is on the verge of dying and if you happen to recognize that person, such a dream foretells a sudden upsurge in your life, but if you do not recognize that person, it forebodes ill health from which you may not recover.

b. You see yourself dying: A serious warning to take care of your health or face the consequences that may place your life in peril.

E

EARRINGS. Earrings symbolize a dreamy nature coupled with difficulties.

a. You see earrings: A pair of golden earrings, whether on your body or in your hands or lying elsewhere, suggests much has to be done to realize your simple goals. Silver ones intensify the difficulties that you will face. With diamonds or any precious stone, it reflects the dreamy nature within you. Be more practical.

b. You buy earrings: A dream foretelling financial problems due to your extravagant behavior.

EARTHQUAKE. Seeing or being told of an earthquake in one's dream is not favorable, since it symbolizes loss, destruction, misery, and even a change of address that may turn out to be too unbearable.

a. You see or are told of an earthquake: Whether you see or are told of an earthquake that has devastated a village or a city, it forebodes problems from various directions; unemployment, domestic problems, usually heated and useless arguments with your spouse, and even a brief but painful health problem.

b. You are in the midst of a devastated region: A city, village, or any residential region devastated by earthquake means you will have to face unbearable problems within the next few weeks that could have great negative effects on your mental bearings. Think wisely and tackle your problems with sagacity, since they will be short-lived. If planning to change your address, refrain from doing so at least for the next forty days.

EATING. Eating in one's dream signifies good health coupled with joy. At the same time, depending on what you are eating, there could be unfavorable significances too.

a. You are eating: If you are eating with friends and the atmosphere appears amicable, it is a sure sign of business success, while eating with your spouse means a well-earned labor and with your parents, it denotes continued good health and happiness together with good relations with them. If you (a married woman) happen to be eating alone in a sad mood, it reflects your wrongdoing against your husband and if unmarried but expecting to marry soon and you have such a dream, it means that you will have a breakage in your relation chiefly due to your dishonest ways in life. If you (a married man) dream of eating alone in a sad mood, it means that you have been wrongly accusing your wife or having doubts about her. But whether married or unmarried and if you happen to be eating alone in a good mood, it means that at least one of your modest projects will materialize very soon much to your satisfaction. If you are married but appear to be eating with a previous friend of the opposite sex, it underscores your angry and uncompromising nature, which will greatly cause you troubles. It also means that you may be to a certain extent unfaithful.

EGGS. Very rarely do we dream of eggs. It may be a single egg or indefinite numbers of them. Some may be cracked or open, others may even have the young ones showing. Essentially there may be a difference in the significance of the eggs belonging to the "fowl family" from that of those belonging to the reptiles, such as turtles, snakes, and alligators. While the former symbolize auspicious developments, the latter may have ominous omens.

a. You see eggs: Chicken eggs suggest you are quite reserved in your plannings and hence will be rewarded for your labors. Duck, goose, swan or any other water fowl eggs herald an end to family disputes and to an extent financial problems. Turkey eggs denote slight inconsistencies that could be rectified with a little thinking. Pigeon eggs reflect your ego and at the same time your laziness. If you see eggs of any of these birds that appear broken, destroyed, or empty, it suggests your inability to apply all your potential due to a nervous disposition. Eggs just hatched with the young ones within (a rare dream) signifies health, wealth, and happiness. Hatched eggs with the chicks dead within the egg shell or lying dead around warn of an illness. Crushed eggs lying around you forebode a general loss unless you move fast enough to prevent it. Rotten eggs symbolize insincere friends who may harm you.

b. You see eggs of reptiles: Intact reptile eggs in any quantity are considered as an exceptionally ominous dream signifying a bad present and future with illness, quarrels, lawsuits, violence, and even bankruptcy. Crushed reptile eggs signify a certain degree of amelioration. Empty reptile eggs forebode violence and conspiracies that could endanger your life. Empty reptile eggs with little ones around them forebode a violent death unless you hasten to take great care. A dead reptile near the egg symbolizes safety and your will to refrain from crime and vice.

EMBALMING. An embalmed animal or a human being in a dream suggests success in business or love affairs. It is also a symbol of continued good health.

a. You see an embalmed human being: If you (a woman) see an embalmed man, it denotes the faithfulness of your husband and if you (a man) see an embalmed woman, it denotes the deep affection you have for your wife. It also suggests a lasting relation with your spouse devoid of any misunderstanding. If you see someone whom you recognize (other than your spouse), it is a sure sign of success in your business undertakings but only if you are in business. If it is your spouse, it means that you have been a professional fraud.

b. You see an embalmed animal or bird: An embalmed cat or dog signifies a contented domestic life whereas any bird signifies good fortune, often a financial breakthrough.

c. You see embalming: Any animal being embalmed signifies financial and health recovery whereas a bird being embalmed suggests a sudden change, often for the better. A human being in the process of being embalmed denotes a long and a healthy life coupled with success.

EMBRACE. Embracing someone in a dream is considered favorable, since it denotes your ability to forget the past.

a. You embrace: If you recognize the person and if you have had some bickerings with him, it is a sure sign that you will both forget the past and if you do not recognize the person in question, it means that very soon you will be mending a hostile relation with someone that has been troubling you. If a friend, it foretells a good business venture and if it is your business partner, it foretells business success. If you appear to embrace your own children, it foretells a very early reconciliation with your spouse if estranged and a compromise with your lover or beloved if temporarily sharing any anger or misunderstanding. If not estranged with your lover or friend and you appear to embrace a child or more, such a dream foretells a unique bondage of friendship with your spouse or lover or friend.

b. You embrace your enemy or someone you detest: Such a dream reflects your hypocritic nature that could cost you much vis-à-vis society. It also means a degradation in general.

EMPLOYER. Depending on the atmosphere, an employer has both a good as well as an unfavorable significance.

a. You see an employer: If you appear to know the employer in question and if unemployed, it is a sign foretelling the end of your unemployment days and if already employed, it could mean a modest promotion or a new job proposal.

b. You see yourself as an employer: This is considered a good dream, signifying you will in the future begin your own business however modest it may be.

ENEMY. An enemy symbolizes nervousness and an angry behavior.

a. You see a former enemy: If you see a former enemy with whom you now share cordial relations, it means you will continue to make mistakes through hasty decisions. If you see someone whom you imagine to be your enemy, it means you are unrealistic. Seeing a person in whom rests enmity for you means unhappiness at home. If you manage to compromise or reconcile, it is a good sign, foretelling an end to bickerings at home and at your place of work.

b. You quarrel with your enemy: Arguing or fighting with your enemy is not auspicious, since it betokens unending hardships, financial loss, and even total isolation.

ESCAPE. The significance of escape in one's dream solely depends on the place of escape and your situation.

a. You escape from imminent danger to your life: A favorable sign promising success if you are able to change your life-style. It also means that you will change your former friends for better ones.

b. You escape from a prison: If you feel that you are being unlawfully held in a prison, it presages a change in your business affairs, which will be for the better. It also means that you will drop your partners, if any, and independently run your own business, which will bring you the desired satisfaction. If you appear to be escaping from a prison where you are being held legally, it means you are heading for a total reversal in life.

EXCREMENT. Excrement in one's dream symbolizes an end to hardships and sufferings.

a. You and excrement: Passing excrement in one's dream symbolizes an early settlement to petty problems. Seeing excrement in a lavatory or on the ground denotes an end is finally coming to your social and mental problems. It also means that you will finally obtain your modest wishes no matter how difficult they appear to you. If you appear to see or feel excrement in your trousers, it means you have had an extremely tense situation with your family members but that you were not aware that it was the exaggeration in your mind that created the unhappiness in you. If you appear to see excrement on the ground or on your body (which is rare), it means all your honest efforts in life will ultimately bear fruits much to your surprise.

b. You appear to eat excrement: A good dream for those in abject poverty. Such a dream also means a sudden help from the most unexpected quarter, which would drastically change your life for the better.

EXECUTION. Execution of a person in a dream symbolizes both favorable as well as unfavorable developments. Depending on who is being executed, several interpretations can be had.

a. You witness an execution: If you recognize the person as an innocent person being executed, it means your activities, whether social or business, will temporarily suffer. If you do not recognize the person being executed, it means uncertainty to your labors. If a known criminal is being executed, it means your labors will finally be rewarded.

b. You are being executed: If you feel that you have already been executed, it means a new beginning in life, which will be much better than you would have expected. It also foretells fame and riches through honest means. If you appear to be readied for execution, it foretells new friends who will be greatly instrumental in your prosperity.

EXILE. An unhappy dream reflecting your unhappiness with society and your deep frustration. This dream has significance for only those in exile from their country.

a. You see yourself in exile: Such a dream foretells a change in your address that will not be to your benefit. It also means that you are too frustrated with friends and acquaintances.

b. Your family members or friends are banished: If you dream that they are beginning their journey into exile, it is a warning to you to be more rational and practical. If you dream that they are already in exile elsewhere, it means more mental tortures as a result of discouragement.

c. You appear to have returned to your own country, although in the conscious state, you are in exile: Such a dream presages that although your present government is cruel and anti-human and is in control of your country, that government will ultimately fall no matter which other power supports that country.

EYES. Seeing or focusing on the eyes in one's dream has several indications both favorable and otherwise.

a. You see eyes: If you appear to focus on the eyes of a person in a dream, you appear to be searching for a fair and honest outlet towards a more meaningful life. If the eyes appear angry or furious, it means your ways of life are not appreciated. If the eyes appear red, swollen, or infected, it means you will soon face a temporary period of setbacks and even ill health.

b. You dream you have lost an eye or both of them: One of the most ominous dreams of all. Such a dream foretells a terrible loss, perhaps a life within the family, usually that of a young person.

F

FACE. Depending on the type of face seen, several interpretations, both favorable as well as unfavorable, can be had.

a. You see a face: If the face is recognized, it denotes a sudden development for the better, but only if it is smiling. If angry, it denotes a short period of uneasiness.

b. You see your own face: If your face appears normal, it signifies an entry into a more meaningful stage in life. If you appear sad, such a dream speaks of the various challenges you will have to face in life and if you appear full of joy, smiling, or even laughing, it means that destiny will assist you to overcome the hurdles in life. If you appear to be criticized, it means that you have to guard your emotions vis-à-vis the jealous persons around you.

FACTORY. A factory denotes hard work, success, and satisfaction in general.

a. You see a factory: A factory in a dream indicates your hard work will finally crown you with success. It also means that you are doing well where employment is concerned. If you see smoke from the chimney of a factory, it is a sure sign of promotion or a better employment proposal.

b. You see yourself in a factory: Such a dream promises a happy social life. It also underscores your desire to earn your own living.

c. You see yourself working in a factory: A wonderful dream foretelling success although modest in virtually all activities you undertake.

FAME. A favorable dream symbolizing opportunities and chances that will make you realize at least a part of your goals.

a. You dream you are famous: If living in modesty and humbleness in true life, it means that there will be a "stepping stone" somewhere in the near future, which will enable you to witness a change for the better even if all the odds appear to be against you at the present. In the same vein, a person with an appreciable economic situation will gain prosperity and further financial success.

b. Any of your family members become famous: Whether your parents, siblings, family members or your spouse, such a dream presages good opportunities that will greatly enhance your life-style.

FAMINE. Contrary to what it implies, famine symbolizes bounty and happy moments.

a. You dream of being famine-stricken: An auspicious dream foretelling better days ahead of you. If at the present you are poverty-stricken, ailing, or separated from your spouse or lover, a general amelioration is in sight.

b. You see a famine-stricken region: If you recognize that region in

82

question, it is an unmistaken sign that you will find prosperity there and if you do not recognize the region, it means you must have patience to see your goals achieved. If you are told that a certain region is famine-stricken, it means that particular place will experience bounty and happiness.

FARM. A farm symbolizes prosperity, respect, and continued friendly relations with those around you.

a. You see a farm: If the farm appears well cared for and in good condition, it denotes prosperity through business. If not involved in business and if employed, it means stability in work. If unemployed but with either an ability to work or with the required qualifications, it means that very soon you will get work of your choice. Be not dismayed.

b. You see yourself on a farm: If you are a writer, a success awaits you and if a businessman, you can expect your business to expand, though not with great financial gains. If you are a farm worker and dream of working on a farm, it is an unmistakable sign that one day, whether sooner or later, you will own your own farm although modest.

c. You see a farm on fire: This is an unpleasant dream, signifying your efforts will be in vain if you fail to see the more practical aspect of life. Channel your abilities and talents in a more practical way.

FATHER. A father in one's dream is a symbol of his genuine love and affection for you. If your father is already dead and he appears to you in your dream, there are several messages for you, depending on the developments in the dream.

a. You see your father: If he is alive, it underscores his great support for you. If he is dead and appears in your dream (and if you are not in a happy situation), it is an advice to rectify your errors. It also means that if you have any pending lawsuit against you and if you feel innocent, the verdict will be in your favor. If you are ill and if you see your father (whether he is dead or living), you will progressively recover. If you are in despair and feel hopeless, you will have brighter days.

b. Your father is dead long ago but in your dream you are unaware: A dead father rarely speaks. If his presence is friendly, it is a good sign, promising peace and calm ahead of you. If he seems unhappy, it foretells sad days ahead of you unless you move wisely. Any gift from a dead father signifies prosperity and happiness, although at a much later stage.

FEATHERS. Depending on the type of the feather, favorable as well as unfavorable significances can be had.

a. You see feathers: If the feathers happen to be white, it denotes a simple and clean life devoid of problems. If black, it indicates the mysterious behavior of acquaintances and even that of family members.

b. You buy or sell feathers: Buying feathers in one's dream signifies loss through fraud by those whom you trust, while selling feathers indicates you are not being too honest. It also means you plan to indulge in unlawful acts.

FIGHTING. Fighting with someone or violence suggests the dreamer is regularly involved in petty quarrels and is short-tempered. It is advice to practice restraint and mend one's character.

a. You are fighting: If you (a married man) appear to be fighting with your wife, it means you are unnecessarily bearing a grudge against her due to your sheer foolish ways of thinking. If you (a woman) appear to be fighting with your husband, it denotes your weakness in understanding your husband. But if you appear to be fighting with your family members, it is a good sign, indicating some financial benefits that they may envy.

b. You are injured while fighting: If you are shot, stabbed, or wounded in any form while fighting, it denotes a general failure in life.

FINGER. A finger has both favorable as well as an unfavorable significance. Depending on the situation of the finger, an interpretation can be had.

a. You see a finger: If a finger appears pointed threateningly or menacingly at you, it means the threats that you have already received appear serious. If the finger appears to be simply pointed at you, it denotes a warning to be more careful. But if the finger appears pointed to you in a friendly manner and has a ring on it and if you recognize that person, it is a symbol of encouragement, which could lead you to better days.

b. You see a severed or a bleeding finger: If it is your own finger, it denotes a general loss, perhaps a heated dispute with your in-laws (if married) and if unmarried a deep misunderstanding with your parents or siblings. A severed or a cut finger belonging to a person whom you do not recognize means jealousies but which could not have any adverse effects on you.

FINGERNAILS. Fingernails in one's dream have a good as well as an unfavorable significance.

a. You see fingernails: If you see your own nails that appear tidy and well kept, it is a sign of good health and mental stability. If they appear untidy, overgrown, or broken, it foretells loneliness and ill health.

b. You are cutting your fingernails: A good dream presaging your entry into a more positive and profitable profession.

c. You see fingernails strewn all over: If you happen to just see them, it means that you are indifferent towards your own future, but if you happen to either stamp your feet on them or clean them away, it means there is an urge within you to do something constructive.

FIRE. Fire in a dream has been considered as an organic dream by the majority of the masters. The significances deemed interpretable are listed below.

a. You see a fire engulfing everywhere: An ominous dream signifying a terrible development affecting your life in general, especially your domestic and social affairs. For all those involved in business or trade, such a dream advocates calm through meditation and prayers. For those desiring to go on a journey however short it may be, it is advisable to postpone it for at least a week. If you happen to see people fighting the blaze, there are chances that the intensity of the bad period will be greatly reduced. If all of a sudden the blaze appears to die out, it means that the dream has no prophetic significance.

b. You see a fire in a fireplace: Such a dream promises warmth and affection for you from the society. For the married, it denotes a complete happiness.

FISH. A fish or several of them in one's dream signifies prosperity in general. It also denotes the realization of one's goals in life.

a. You see fish: If you see a single fish in the water and if the fish happens to look at you, it is a sure sign that destiny will eventually smile on you. If the fish is just seen, it means you will not be disappointed in your simple goals. Fish seen on a dry surface denote a temporary anger within you, which will pass away with time. If you see several of them in the water and if you happen to either feed them or they appear to stay where you are, it is a sure sign of assistance from trustworthy friends but not family members. If you manage to touch any of the fish, it is a good sign of prosperity in a far-off land.

b. You eat fish: Eating fish in one's dream signifies a marked amelioration in life. If you find yourself in a fish market, it means that you will have a fruitful journey.

FISHING. Fishing in one's dream signifies a search for a new life.

a. You see yourself fishing: This is a dream encouraging you to continue your efforts. If you are successful in angling a fish, it means there is every possibility to attain your goals provided honesty and decency are your prime principles. If you fall in the water while fishing, it means you are still unprepared to begin seeking your goals and hence need more careful planning.

b. You see others fishing: Such a dream asks you to consider one or more of your successful friends as an example and follow in his footsteps.

FLAG. Anything resembling a flag in one's dream signifies honor.

a. You see a flag: If you are able to identify the flag, it denotes a forthcoming promotion (if you are employed) or success in election (if you are running for any official post). If you see an alien flag in your dream, it means that you will travel abroad for some important business affair that may turn out to be in your favor. If you see your own country's flag torn or thrown on the ground, it foretells a period of hardships. Tearing or dishonoring your own national flag reflects your ingrate behavior vis-à-vis your friends, family members, and virtually all those around you.

b. You are presented a flag: A good sign signifying people's approval of your presence in society.

FLOODS/FLOODING. A flood in a dream usually signifies setbacks, since it is often associated with devastation and destruction.

a. You see floods: An inauspicious dream foretelling business and financial setbacks. If houses appear to be flooded, it means an undesired misunderstanding within the family, often ending in unhappiness for all.

b. You see a desert flooded: This is a good sign, denoting prosperity and happiness after long years of hardships and difficulties.

c. You find yourself within a flood: An unfavorable dream signifying future unhappiness as a result of your past unlawful activities.

FLYING (you are physically flying). Flying in one's dream is considered auspicious.

a. You appear to be flying: A wonderful dream signifying wealth, health, and prosperity in general. If you are flying quite high from the ground, you will attain your goals within one calendar year, but if flying low, the period of attaining your goals will be delayed.

b. You see others flying: A good dream encouraging you to go ahead with your plans, since even though you may not have a great degree of success, you will not experience a loss.

FOREST. A forest symbolizes the unknown.

a. You see a forest: Seeing a forest from a distance foretells uncertainty to your projects. It also means that you are doing things at the behest of others. Be more practical and cautious.

b. You are in a forest: If you see yourself alone in a forest but you appear to know your way out, it means although at the present you are undergoing a difficult period, you will finally see satisfaction. But if you appear lost, it means you appear to need professional help to realize your projects.

FORT. A fort is a symbol of dignity, power, and determination.

a. You see a fort: If the fort appears to be well-maintained, it is a symbol of your strong will power and determination to live in dignity whatever the results may be. But if the fort appears to be in ruins with overgrown vegetation around it, it foretells uncertainty to your plans.

b. You are inside a fort: A good sign indicating you will receive all the needed support. It also means that if you are a writer or a researcher or even in the educational profession, your efforts will be crowned with success.

c. You see a fort overrun or occupied: If the invaders around the fort are violent, it means a conspiracy is already hatched against you, but if they appear friendly, it means you have erred in judging your acquaintances.

FOUNTAIN. A fountain chiefly symbolizes good health.

a. You see a fountain: If the fountain spouts clean water, it foretells prosperity and good health. It is also a sign of pure love. Drinking water from the fountain regardless of the quality of the water means financial prosperity and domestic satisfaction. A broken or an abandoned fountain symbolizes delays, which may cause you financial problems.

FRIENDS. The presence of friends symbolizes support. Rarely does a friend speak much in a dream.

a. You see your friend: If you see your former friend who is far away from you, it means you feel lonely and believe you lack moral support. If that friend and you exchange embraces, it means you will very soon find a friend with whom you will share cordial relations. If you see a person whom you no more consider as your friend and if that person or you exchange a heated argument, it means the nervousness within you still exists. But if you both engage in a friendly conversation, it means you are still hesitant and undecided.

FRONTIER. Crossing a frontier or seeing one symbolizes your urgent desire to enter a new phase in life.

a. You are at the frontier: Seeing a frontier of two countries or states but feeling unable to cross it means you have certain difficulties that have been chiefly created by others. Reticence and patience will ultimately help you overcome your problems.

b. You appear to be crossing a frontier: If you happen to be contemplating immigrating to another part of the world and if you appear to have crossed the frontier with ease, it is a sure sign that you will have a much better life in the new country of your choice, but if you are stopped, prevented, or subjected to embarrassing interrogations, it means that you have wrongly chosen to immigrate. If one or more officials at the frontier help you to "slip" across the frontier, it means a last-minute support from unknown sources will help you realize your goals.

FUNERAL. Funerals in one's dream symbolize the end of a particular cycle or journey in life and the beginning of a new profession in trade, usually in another location. They also symbolize success.

a. You see a funeral: If you happen to recognize the dead person in the funeral procession, that person will have a new beginning in life essentially for the better. If you do not recognize and you appear to be simply standing there watching the funeral pass by, it means that very soon you will embark on an ambitious project if in business, or successfully pass an examination or test or win a pending lawsuit. If you happen to be among the crowd, a sudden change in life is expected whether for the better or otherwise. Seeing a funeral pyre being lit is a sure sign of change in address, usually for the better.

b. You participate in your own funeral: Such a dream has several significances: if unmarried you may suddenly find your future bride. If unemployed or in poverty, there are chances of better days and if someone asks you to participate in your own funeral or tells you that he has already participated in your funeral, it indicates the end of a bitter period for you.

G

GALLOWS. Depending on the situation, several interpretations can be had.

a. You see gallows: Just seeing gallows is a strong warning to immediately discontinue relations with those persons whose confidence you doubt. If you see several persons standing or sitting near the gallows, it means that although you have had several warnings and admonishments from various persons to tread on the right path, you have been arrogant to do as you please. Practice constraint from vice through prayers.

b. You are led to the gallows: This is a contrary dream signifying the end to your miseries in general. It also spells the beginning of a new and a fruitful life marked by appreciable joy. If you see persons accompanying you to the gallows, it means that you will have new and good friends. If someone tells you that you must hurry and if you appear frightened, it means that you are worrying too much about things that are in reality minor and unworthy to note.

c. You escape from the gallows: If you appear to escape while being led to the gallows, it is a good sign that you will be forgiven for your wrongdoings, if any.

d. You see a person being led to the gallows: Such a dream forebodes betrayal by your wife. Do not confront her but closely control her activities and guard yourself well against any of her evil acts.

GAMES. Depending on what game is being played, several significances can be had.

a. You are playing a game alone: If you appear to be playing with a deck of cards (whether alone or with others), it is a harbinger of bad financial situation. Any other game, such as building blocks or any educational game, means that you are trying to stay away from burdensome acquaintances.

b. You are playing games with others: Playing football (soccer) denotes your desire to have a good business partner or dependable friends, while playing hockey (on ice or on grass) denotes an earnest desire to enter into business, which will fortunately be realized although at a later stage. Playing dice, chinese checkers, chess, backgammon, tests of knowledge and education, in short, any game requiring two, means there are many possibilities within the next two weeks, fortnights, or months whereby you will receive the positive results of your labors, but only if you have performed the required acts whose results you expect, two or more months ago.

GARDEN. The ancient proverb is, "A garden is a place where God wrought." It is considered a symbol of joy and happiness fountaining from a happy marriage. Hence this dream is for those either on the verge of being married or those married. For the unmarried and chronic bachelors, this dream has no significance.

a. You and a garden: If the garden appears well kept and beautiful

91

and if you are planning to marry, it is an assurance of a happy marriage and if you are already married, it means that you will be blessed with good children. But if the garden appears unkempt, in shambles and overgrown, it means there will be several serious setbacks to your married life as a result of minor misunderstandings. If you happen to see ruins where once stood a beautiful garden, it means the end of the short period of unhappiness within your family. If you happen to be walking in the garden either in the company of your spouse, your family members or friends, it means that you will soon meet with a sudden success that will surprise you.

GARDENER. A gardener symbolizes peace, love, affection, and sympathy. As such, it is considered as a favorable dream. It is suggested that the "haves" usually dream of a garden.

a. You see a gardener: If you see any of your family member who has suddenly become a gardener, it means that person will reach a certain position in life where he will help the needy and those in distress. If you recognize the person as a gardener (in the conscious state), it means that you are contemplating on exchanging your materialistic life for a spiritual life.

b. You are a gardener: If you dream you are gardening, it means that before you pass or end your earthly cycle of life, you will be able to realize the most ambitious goal you have: to serve others. A wonderful dream indeed. If someone appears to criticize you while you are gardening, it means that you have jealous persons around you while if you appear praised, it means that you have the support of well-wishers.

GATE. A gate in a dream is a symbol of hope. This is a dream usually dreamt by those harboring the welfare of others while having a strong belief in the Creator of the Universe. A dream for those spiritually inclined.

a. You see a gate: A gate believed to be that of a fort or a palace generally means that your prayers to serve others will be answered by the Lord of the Universe. If the gate appears closed, it means that those who have harmed you or others and whose salvation you seek will be ultimately realized. But if the gates appear open, it means that your sacrifices in life have not been in vain. If you appear to see the gates overgrown by weeds or vegetation, it means that you yourself have not been too serious during a certain period of your earthly life. If you appear to be cleaning or cutting the overgrown vegetation or clearing the entrance, it means that you have been making efforts, although not with a full heart.

b. You see a destroyed gate or one in ruins: Such a dream means you have erred somewhere in life, perhaps lived the life of a hypocrite in the past, which you regret. Prayers, meditation, and trust in the Lord will deliver you.

GHOST. A "ghost" in one's dream has several significances, both favorable as well as otherwise. In case the dreamer is sick, has fever, or appears frightened, such a dream has no significance for him.

a. You see a ghost: If the "ghost" appears to frighten or threaten you and then passes by, it means that doubts within you concerning your present activities are incorrect. If the ghost appears unfriendly, it indicates coming setbacks in matrimonial and financial affairs.

b. A ghost gives you something or speaks to you: If the ghost gives you something, it means that you will get rid of your ugly past, but if he asks you something, it means that you will continue to have a period marked by problems.

GIANT. A giant in one's dream is both auspicious as well as otherwise. Any abnormally huge person may be considered a giant.

a. You see a giant: If the giant appears friendly, it is a sure sign of good support for you in the society, but if he appears angry or threatening, it means you will have quarrels with your superiors either at your place of work or your parents. If the giant appears to advise you, it is a clear sign of help from influential persons.

b. You are a giant: If you dream that you have suddenly become a giant or a person physically towering over others around you, it means you will arrive at a right conclusion within the next few days that would immensely please you.

GIRL. A young girl has both a favorable as well as an unfavorable significance in life. Depending on her situation vis-à-vis yours, an interpretation can be had.

a. You see a girl: If the girl is known to you and if she appears smiling, friendly, or affectionate towards you, it is a sign of general success to your labors in life, thanks to your honesty. If you do not know the girl and if she is very appealing to you in terms of her childish beauty and charm, it means you will have a new love affair. If the girl appears untidy, crying, angry or abusive, it means that you will have a misunderstanding with your spouse over unnecessary subjects. Be more sagacious and understanding.

b. You (a woman) become a girl: If you are unmarried and you dream of becoming a girl, it means that you will marry sooner or later, whatever your age, your physical description, or your situation in general may be. It also means that you will marry a person much younger than you. If you are married and you have bickerings with your husband, it means that you will have a peaceful divorce to the satisfaction of both. If happily married and you dream of becoming a girl, it means continued good health, health recovery if ailing, and financial recovery if in difficulties.

c. You threaten or beat a girl: This is an ominous sign, foretelling an accident that may temporarily impair your health. Refrain from long journeys for about a fortnight. Act prudently.

GIRL FRIEND. Depending on whether she is your former girl friend or a present one and depending on her situation and yours, several significances can be had.

a. You and the girl friend: Seeing your former girl friend in an emotional atmosphere underscores your ever-lasting sadness of missing her but only if she has left you. If you were responsible for the separation, it means that you still regret the situation. But if the atmosphere is not emotional for both of you and appears normal and if you think or know that she bears grudge against you in her conscious state and that she was the one who created the separation, it means she was not in the least worthy of your friendship. If she appears to cry uncontrollably, it means that within her heart she still bears affection for you. Seeing your current girl friend denotes a good future for both, but only if she does not anger, accuse, or torment you. If she happens to give you a small gift or present, it underlies her real love.

GLOVES. Gloves symbolize care and reticence in one's activities. Depending on other developments with gloves, other significances can be had.

a. You and gloves: If you appear to be wearing a pair of gloves regardless of their type and the weather, it denotes the importance of care and reticence you attach to your daily activities. If you (a man) are given a pair of gloves by a woman you know, it reflects the strong affection within her for you and if you do not recognize her, it means you are simply unaware of what you are doing. If a man presents you (a woman) with a pair of gloves and whether you recognize that person or not and if you are married, it denotes a stormy period with your husband and if unmarried with virtually all those around you. Practice patience and calm through prayers. Buying gloves again means your reticence. Finding some means good advice while losing them signifies your irreverence towards life. Holding a single glove in hand or wearing a single one denotes you are undecided and need advice.

GRAIN. Any type of eatable grain in one's dream foretells joy, abundance, and good health.

a. You see grain: If in sacks and piled all around you in a warehouse or in a shop, it is a clear sign of abundance if you are a farmer. If not a farmer, you can expect joyous news, a good development in the family, a marriage or a reconciliation among feuding family members. Grain appearing to be strewn on the ground reflects your reckless behavior and your failure to grasp the good opportunities. But if you happen to see someone collecting the strewn grains or you yourself appear to be collecting them, it is a sign denoting your will to be more serious and responsible.

GRASS. Depending on the situation, grass has several significances, both favorable as well as otherwise.

a. You and grass: If you appear to be standing in the midst of grass and if the grass appears fresh and green, it indicates energy and good health within you, but if the grass appears pale or dried up, it means you are headed for a temporary setback in financial affairs. Seeing fresh and green grass from a distance will greatly ease your mental woes. If you appear to be mowing or cutting grass, it means that a rural life appears to be more beneficial to you, since you are easily agitated with people around you. But if you appear to be cutting or mowing the grass of a friend or someone asks you to do this for him or her, it means that an urban life promises more happiness for you, since it would be there where you will be able to prove your mettle.

GRAVE. A grave symbolizes justice, hope, and good news.

a. You see a grave (not related to your kin): Whether an imposing or a simple one, a grave is a symbol of hope for the hopeless and those in despair. It also means that justice, although delayed, will not be ultimately denied. If you are expecting an answer to any request, the response will greatly please you, although it will take some time.

b. You see a grave (those belonging to family members or friends): If you see the grave of your father, it means you will have support, while that of your mother symbolizes encouragement. Your son's symbolizes your deep emotions and your desire to shun falsehood and crime while your daughter's reflects your desire to begin a settled life. Graves of siblings reflect the urge within you to face the challenges in life with honesty. A friend's grave reminds you that crime will not pay while an enemy's denotes peace and calm within you.

GROCER. A grocer in a dream reflects hard work and even risks in life. Depending on the situation of the grocer and you, several of their significances can be seen.

a. You see a grocer: If he happens to be your local grocer and if he greets you or gives you some good news, it means that you must continue to persevere hard in life to achieve your goals, but if he gives you any unpleasant news, it is a sure sign of problems that require sorting out.

b. You are in a grocery: If you buy something in a grocery, it means that you are on the right track of life, but if you happen to just stand or watch things in a grocery, it means that you are idly passing your time without any constructive plans. If you find yourself unable to pay for things that you have purchased in a grocery, it means you are depending too much on false hopes.

c. You quarrel with a grocer: If you know the grocer, it means that you are quite careful. It also means that you will be successful in business. If you do not know the grocer, it means that you will not take any risks in your life.

GUN. A gun (rifle, revolver, or any object that fires a projectile) in one's dream symbolizes uncertainty and unreliable temper. Depending on your situation vis-à-vis the weapon, several other significances can be had.

a. You and a gun: Having a gun either in your hand or with you underscores your easily agitated temper. If you appear to threateningly point it at someone, it means that you are responsible for your present woes. If you appear to be holding a gun at your spouse, it means that you are too nervous, while at your children, it means that you are not being too serious with them. If at your parents, it means that you detest society in general.

b. Someone holds a gun on you: If it happens to be your wife, it means that she is an outright fraud and a woman who will leave no stones unturned to rob you. If she happens to be a second wife and if she happens to have several children from her first or previous other marriages, it is a sure sign that she is out to ruin you while covertly serving the interests of her children. Get rid of that snake of a woman. If your parents or siblings happen to hold a gun at you, it is a reminder that a serious approach to life will ultimately lead to your prosperity.

GYPSY. A Gypsy symbolizes wandering, instability, and restlessness.

a. You see a Gypsy: One or more of them either camped or in the open implies a continued period of wandering and restlessness. If the Gypsy nears you or even speaks to you, regardless of the topic of conversation, it means you will very soon change your residence and perhaps your place of employment.

b. You quarrel with a Gypsy: Quarrelling with a Gypsy forebodes general problems arising from a trip you have in mind. Postpone the trip if any for at least a fortnight. If the Gypsy promises you good luck in return for money, it means that you must beware of false friends. If you refuse to pay him or ignore him, it is a good sign denoting success in general. If you attack or beat or drive away a Gypsy, it denotes the deep degree of restlessness within you.

H

HAIL. Hail or hailstorm are usually associated with a sudden turn for the worse, mostly concerned with business and social affairs. As such, it is considered as an unfavorable dream.

a. You see hailstorms: If you see it over a city, it denotes that your new business deal will not be successful. If it hails over a village or over the countryside, it speaks of a financial loss. If it hails over a lake or a stretch of water, it foretells illness or worsening of health (if you are already ill), but if it hails over the desert, it signifies a sudden change in your life that may be more for the better and less for the worse.

b. You are caught in a hailstorm: A strong warning to disown your acquaintances who have already brought you enough misery. For a married man, it is a strong warning to beware of his wife's movements and for a woman, it means that her husband is treading the wrong path in society. If you appear to have great difficulty walking in the hailstorm, it means that it will take some time until you will be able to find a calm period.

HAIR. The significance of hair in a dream depends on the situation of the hair. Accordingly, depending on its characteristics, several significances can be had.

a. You and the hair: If your hair in the conscious state is gray or white and you dream that it has become brown or black, it means that you are progressively regaining your vitality, and if it appears abnormally long, it means that you will also recoup your other shortcomings. If your hair is already black or brown in your conscious state and you dream that it has grayed, it means that you have not taken enough care of your health. If you dream that your hair has become either golden or red, it underlines your hypocritic nature.

HALO. A halo symbolizes spiritual gains. It also symbolizes health recovery.

a. You see a halo: If it appears on your parents, it is a promise of a long and a healthy life for them while if on your siblings, it means that you will all be blessed with a meaningful and a spiritual life. If any of your family members is ill and if a person with a halo on him tells you that he will recover, it is a sure sign of recovery. If someone tells you that you have a halo on your head, it means you will be deceived into entering a business venture that will bring you loss and if you see a halo on a woman, it means you will be tricked by a woman who will be at least a day older than you.

HAMMER. A hammer in a dream symbolizes hard work, honesty, and modest success. Depending on what the hammer is used for, other significances can be had.

a. You are using a hammer: If you are using a hammer for construction purposes, it symbolizes a modest financial gain while hammering a nail on a door suggests that you are unawaredly blocking your own path to progress. If you are using a hammer to give shape to any metal object, it means that your honest labors will ultimately materialize. If you appear to be using a hammer to break any object, it reflects uncertainty in your business affairs. If you appear to threaten someone with a hammer, it means that your nervousness will cause you problems.

b. You are threatened with a hammer: If you know that person, it means that jealousies in the family will cause you hardships unless you tackle them with care. If you do not recognize the person, it means that some form of conspiracy is going on against you.

HANDS. Hands symbolize messages to oneself both favorable as well as otherwise.

a. You see your right hand: Since the right hand represents your spouse and children (if married) and your present activities and if it appears clean and lively, it foretells a happy married life for those yet unmarried and a complete family concord for those married. For those never desiring to marry, it means spiritual gains. A dirty and deformed-looking hand denotes disappointment and setbacks.

b. You see your left hand: The left hand represents your family, parents, and siblings. If it appears clean and lively, it means perfect relations with all of them while if untidy or deformed, it means continued bickerings with them.

c. You see a child's hand: A child's hand, whether dirty or clean, presages a total change in your life for the better.

HANGING. Since hanging ends in death and thus suggests an end to a particular cycle in life on earth and the beginning of another, it is usually considered a favorable dream.

a. You see yourself hanging: If you see yourself being hanged and find that you are still alive, it means that you still have a chance to replan your goals. If you appear already hanged, it means that you will have to continue the ideals and goals that you have already set for yourself but with care.

b. You see others hanging: If it is your father, whether he is alive or dead in his conscious state, it means that you will have the same honor and respect as him from the society and family members. If it is your mother, it means a lot of respect for you.

HAT. Depending on the situation of the hat vis-à-vis your actions, several significances can be had.

a. You have a hat: If you appear to be wearing a hat and if you are pleased, it means that you will have a sudden financial gain, but if you appear sad or angry, it means that you will be the victim of fraud. Similarly, if you appear to be walking at leisure with your hat in your hands, it means that you will soon realize the fruits of your labors, but if you appear disgusted, sad, or angry and appear to be holding your hat in your hand, it means that the business venture that you plan to enter into will not be as successful as you expect.

b. You are given a hat: If someone is in the act of giving you a hat, it means that you deserve the fruits of your labors while if you appear to snatch a hat from anyone, it means that you are contemplating some vicious acts that will greatly endanger your safety.

c. You buy a hat: Buying a hat in one's dream foretells problems and disappointments in marital life. If not married it forebodes misunderstandings with acquaintances.

HAY. Hay denotes the successful realization of a project.

a. You see hay: If you see hay spread around you, it indicates you are on the right path to achieve your goals. If the hay appears in stacks, it is a harbinger of good news.

b. You see hay on fire: A warning to stop depending too much on your friend's advice and to act independently. If people are seen fighting the blaze, it denotes that you will have trustworthy friends. If someone calls you to help fight the blaze, it means that your efforts will materialize soon where you will witness the satisfactory end to your projects and goals.

HEAD. A head in a dream has several significances, favorable as well as otherwise. Depending on the situation, several interpretations can be had.

a. You see a head: If the head appears smiling and friendly, it is a promise of better times. If the head appears unhappy or appears bruised, it is a sign of misfortunes usually caused by a woman. If the head appears menacing, it is a warning to refrain from undesired adventures, since it would lead you to further miseries.

b. You see a severed head: If there is blood around it, the dream is organic and has no prophetic significance, but if the head appears simply severed, it is a harbinger of unhappy news, perhaps the death of a family member.

c. You see your own head: If it is severed, it means enemies posing as friends surround you. If it appears normal, you will receive honors.

HEARSE. A hearse symbolizes a sudden change in one's life.

a. You see a hearse: If the hearse appears to move towards the direction of your house, it is a sign of unexpected gains. If you simply happen to see a hearse pass by, it signifies a joyful period with assistance from acquaintances.

b. You see hearse carrying a family member: Whether your parents, your spouse or friends, a hearse carrying any one of them presages a new beginning for you all.

HELL. Any place in a dream representing what could be termed as "hell" denotes a juncture where a person's life could be changed for the better. It also has unfavorable significances.

a. You see "hell": Seeing yourself within "hell" means it is the right time to begin a meaningful life with a strong determination. If you appear to be "burning" there, it means the strong emotional stress is finally getting the best of you. It also means that your conscience is not at ease for the untoward acts you have committed in the past. If you manage to escape the place, it means that through your labors, you will be able to get rid of your present unpleasant situation. If you see friends or family members in "hell," it means that you are still unaware of the problems you will have to face because of conspiracies already hatched against you.

HERBS. An auspicious dream symbolizing happiness, financial recovery, good health, and an end to family feuds.

a. You see fresh herbs: If the ground around you is full of herbs, it symbolizes absolute happiness. If the herbs appear to be tied in bundles, it signifies either continued good health or recovery for those ailing. For the unemployed it means a job proposal within forty days.

b. You are offered herbs: If the herbs appear fresh, it signifies good news and even an end to family feuds if they exist. Eating fresh or dried herbs that have been offered to you underscores your keen interest in education and sciences.

c. You sell or buy herbs: Selling herbs reflects your desire to help those around you while buying them means you will make concentrated efforts to solve pending problems.

HILLS. A hill or a range of hills symbolizes a challenge in life. Only those with lofty plans have such dreams. A businessman's dream.

a. You see a hill: If you see a single hill, it means you have to cross a few barriers. More of them add to the complexities of the barriers. If recently you have entered into a new business venture and you see a hill, it means although there will be a delay, the result and benefits of your investment will greatly please you.

b. You appear to stand on top of a hill: If a businessman, no matter whether you have been having a difficult period, a setback, or a petty loss, there is every indication that your future deals will turn out to be profitable thanks to your honest ways in life.

HONEY. Honey symbolizes good health, modesty, hard work, and truth.

a. You see honey: If you see honey in a honey comb, it underscores your honest ways in life. Honey in jars or bottles speak of a modest and a contented life whereas finding yourself taking honey from a comb presages the realization of your modest goals within the next few weeks.

b. You eat honey: Such a dream underscores your strong desire to remain fiercely independent. If you see others eating honey with you, it denotes success if you enter into a modest joint business venture. Offering honey to people suggests your shyness while if you are offered honey, it means there are several avenues open to you to achieve your goals.

HORNS. Human "horns" symbolize fraud, evil intentions, and hypocrisy. Animal horns symbolize good luck and prosperity.

a. You have "horns," much to your surprise: Horns, whether well grown or just showing on your head, reflects the deep dishonesty within you. If someone tells you that you have horns whereas you do not appear to see them, it means it is a direct warning to immediately stop your fraudulent ways in life or face legal proceedings. If you see anyone whom you recognize to have horns, it means that person will eventually fall in disgrace.

b. You see animal horns: A goat's horn signifies riches either through inheritance or a costly gift. A cow's horn signifies expansion in business while a sheep's horn means good news is on the way. Horns strewn all over or hung on a wall warns you to refrain from too much extravagance.

HOSPITAL. A hospital symbolizes good health and an end to a period of depression.

a. You see a hospital: If you are sick in your conscious state and see a hospital, it means you will at least partially recover. Being inside the hospital means you are on the verge of recovery only if you are not ailing from any terminal illness. Leaving a hospital means good health and a calm period.

b. You see a makeshift or a field hospital: This is not a favorable dream, since it forebodes accident, illness, or a natural catastrophe, such as a drought, tremor, or floods in your vicinity.

HOUSE. A house symbolizes improvement in living standards, mental calm, and your personal ability to overcome difficulties.

a. You see a house: If it is the one you once owned, it reflects your continued regrets at having sold or parted with it. If it is the house you now own, it symbolizes a better standard of living. If you do not have or never had a house and dream of owning a house, it foretells better days and perhaps a modest house of your own if you keep up your lawful aspirations in life.

b. You see yourself in a house with your spouse or family members: A good dream that presages mental calm after a long period of depression. It also means tolerance and understanding within the family. If you speak to them about buying a house, it is a sure sign that you will buy one within a calendar year.

HUMILIATION. To be humiliated in a dream signifies the contrary. It speaks of respect and honors.

a. You appear to be humiliated: Such a dream means those conspiring or jealous of you will ultimately value your presence in society. This means you will also have honors.

b. You humiliate others: If you appear to humiliate your friends, it signifies your pride and ego. If you appear to humiliate a woman, it means in your conscious state you will learn to respect women. If you appear to be humiliating your spouse, it means you will have lasting relations with her.

HUNCHBACK. A hunchback symbolizes a modest life devoid of vice. It also signifies good news.

a. You see a hunchback: If you know the hunchback or he happens to be a member of your family, it means you will have a modest and a contented life but only if you do not embarrass or quarrel with him. If you do not know the hunchback, it means you will have a sinless life devoid of the least vice. If the hunchback speaks to you in a friendly manner, it means you will receive a positive reply to your requests, but if you happen to quarrel with him, it means that you will continue to have hardships and setbacks due to your own faults. Embracing or being embraced by a hunchback promises a long period of happiness. If he gives you bad news, it is a sure sign of brewing problems from your spouse or friends.

b. You are a hunchback: Such a dream underscores your voracious behavior and greed for more, which will ultimately destroy your mind and body. It is also suggested to be an alcoholic's dream.

HUNGER. A contrary dream for the poor. For the rich it depends on the situation of the dreamer.

a. You dream you are hungry: If you are a poor person and dream of being hungry and even though you have not eaten on the night of the dream, it means that the next few days will be full of surprises where you will receive all the minimum help and assistance from the society. If you are a well-to-do person with a sufficient income and you dream of being hungry in your dream, it means that you are still not content with what you have. But if you are a businessman and you dream of being hungry in your dream, it means there are certain impending problems that you have to sort, which if not resolved could cost you greatly.

b. Your children appear hungry: If your child or children appear hungry and you appear helpless to do something for them, it means that you will not be forgotten by your dependable friends in your hour of need.

HUNTING. Hunting has a good as well as a bad significance. Depending on what is being hunted, an interpretation can be had.

a. You are hunting: If you appear to be invited for a hunt, it means you will receive good news that will radically change your life. If you appear to be either hunting alone or with friends and your aim is to hunt game animals, such as a deer, ibex, rabbit or a boar, it means that you have a constructive approach to life that will help you arrive at your goals in life. If you appear to be hunting dangerous animals, such as a leopard, tiger or a bear, it reflects your courage to overcome difficulties and challenges with wisdom. Hunting birds shows your undependable nature. If you have hunted any pregnant animal, it denotes your cruel and immoral character.

HUSBAND. A husband has several significances, favorable as well as otherwise. Depending on the husband's situation vis-à-vis you (the wife), several significances can be had.

a. You see your husband: If you see your husband accusing, shouting, or questioning your acts, it means that you have not perceived enough to make him understand his own shortcomings. If you are a dependable wife devoid of fraud, it means any outstanding issue will be solved within a very short period to the satisfaction of both. But if you are fraudulent in the conscious state and work against him in private, it means that your husband will eventually leave you for a better life. If your husband appears happy and pleased with you, it means things will greatly ameliorate in your life, thanks to your wisdom.

b. You see someone you desire as a husband: If that person is already married, it has no significance but if he tells you that he will be your husband and if you are married, it means that you are an ingrate vis-à-vis your husband.

c. You attack or confront or argue with your husband: It is suggested that any woman arguing, attacking, or behaving violently with her husband means that she is nervous, undecided, and undependable.

HYMNS. Religious hymns symbolize a life full of virtue. They also symbolize compassion and love for the underprivileged.

a. You are singing hymns: Such a dream underscores your selfless character. If others appear singing with you, it denotes your willingness to go to the farthest point to help the destitute. If you see your family members singing hymns, it means all of you have compassion and love for others while if it is your spouse or children, it denotes your happily married life.

I

ICE. Ice in whatever shape denotes financial loss, quarrels, and misunderstandings within the family. It also denotes illness.

a. You see ice: If you see a vast expanse full of hardened ice, it foretells loss in business. It also suggests risks if you further continue the present profession that you have. If you happen to stand on an icy expanse, it forebodes illness, though you may recover soon. Large chunks of ice denotes living in an unrealistic world, while small ice cubes or pieces seen floating on a small pool or pond are a harbinger of petty quarrels, which may ultimately be solved.

b. You see floating ice: Seeing large chunks of ice floating on a stretch of water or on a river signifies a temporary setback in life as a result of continuous disputes between you and your spouse. Such a dream also spells a bitter separation, often ending in divorce.

IDOLS. Idols in one's dreams symbolize false hopes and an unrealistic approach to life. They also reflect the strong materialistic nature of a person.

a. You see idols around you: Such a dream suggests your desire to arrive at certain strange goals in life and that too without any efforts. It also means that there is an inner urge within you to indulge in fraudulent means. If the idols are of stone, it means you are a petty fraud. Golden or silver idols indicate your unfair activities in life in cooperation with a gang of professional cheats.

b. You appear praying in front of an idol: Such a dream underscores your materialistic nature. It also suggests your character to go to any point in life and face any risk to have fame and riches. Breaking an idol foretells you will eventually return to the right path in life.

ILLNESS. Illness in one's dream symbolizes a long and a healthy life.

a. You appear ill: If you are really ill and you dream of your illness, it foretells an early partial recovery. If you are not ill and have such a dream, it suggests continued good health.

b. You see others ill: If your parents appear ill, such a dream foretells a long life for them. If your spouse or children appear ill, it spells tranquillity and happiness at home. If you see a person you dislike as being ill, it presages a friendly reconciliation. If you see any of your friends as being ill, it suggests a strong bond of friendship between you and them.

INFIDELITY. A contrary dream symbolizing faithfulness in friendship and relations.

a. You behave or act in an unfaithful manner: Such a dream underscores your faithful, honest, and even humble ways in life. It also means that you will never give in to perverted temptations. It also underscores your fierce fidelity towards your spouse, children, and those with whom you deal in life.

b. You see others as being or acting in an unfaithful manner: If it is your spouse, it means your bonds will ever strengthen; if it is your children, it speaks of their great love for you. If unmarried and you happen to see your future spouse as being unfaithful, it speaks of the great devotion and love for you.

INGOT. Ingots have a good as well as unfavorable significances. Depending on their type, an interpretation can be had.

a. You see ingots: A gold one indicates an important development for those in business. For the unemployed, it indicates an early possibility of employment. A sick person dreaming of a gold ingot means he will definitely have at least a partial recovery. An expecting mother dreaming of a gold ingot suggests a healthy child. A silver ingot symbolizes fraud in one's life. A non-precious metal ingot symbolizes hardships in life.

109

b. You and an ingot: Holding a gold ingot suggests time is on your side while holding a silver one means you will have dependable partners in business. Buying a gold ingot symbolizes your insatiable greed for more while buying a silver one reflects your contented nature. Attempting to steal an ingot means you are unsure of your own plans in life.

INK. Ink symbolizes both a favorable as well as an unfavorable development.

a. You see ink: Ink spilt on the ground or paper denotes good news. It also suggests a gift or present from a family member. An ink stain on your body foretells temporary hardships. If the stain appears on your face, it means futile attempts are being made to tarnish your image. Ink stains on hands betokens a financial loss as well as bad health. Ink in a bottle means you will shortly embark on a new plan in life.

b. You buy or make ink: Making ink denotes your desire to enter the world of literary arts as well as your determination to tackle the difficulties of life alone, while buying ink denotes a delayed success in life.

INSANITY. Insanity in one's dream has a favorable as well as an unfavorable significance.

a. You are insane: If you dream you are insane while in life you are planning to marry, it presages a successful marriage. If already married, it means a total concord with your spouse marked with mutual respect. If you find yourself insane at the place of your work, it speaks of impending domestic troubles with your employer. If you find yourself in a state of insanity at home, it speaks of misunderstandings with your spouse. If you appear insane in front of your friends, it foretells arguments with them.

b. Others appear insane to you: If it is your spouse, it means painful arguments leading to deep misunderstandings. If your parents appear insane, it means you have not been too serious in life. If either your brothers or sisters appear insane, it means you are being too conceited in life. If your friends appear insane, it denotes their superficial friendship with you. If any of your family members appear insane, it speaks of impending quarrels and animosities within the family.

INSULT. Insulting someone or being insulted in one's dream symbolizes a weak character and lack of determination. It also speaks of emotional disturbances.

a. You insult someone: If you recognize the person you are insulting, it symbolizes your revengeful character. But if you do not identify your victim, it means you are suffering from nervousness and a state of agitation. If you (a woman) insult another woman, it underscores your jealous nature. But if you insult a person of the opposite sex, it means you are not being too serious in life. If you (a man) insult an old man or a woman, it denotes your lack of confidence and determination in life.

b. Others insult you: If insulted by your father or mother, it is a warning to be more realistic in life. If insulted by your spouse, it speaks of your reckless behavior. If insulted by friends, it means you are not too honest in life.

INTERVIEW. An interview in a dream has various significances, depending on your situation vis-à-vis the interviewer.

a. You have an interview: If you are being interviewed by an employer, it only serves to stress the importance you attach to employment. If you are being interviewed by a writer, it reflects your desire for some prominence in society. If a schoolteacher is interviewing you, it means you are continuously worried about an evaluation test in your work (if employed) or related to seeking employment. If a judicial official appears to interview you, it speaks of doubts within you. If the police appear to interview you, it signifies impending problems with the law. If a doctor appears to be questioning you on your health, it betokens ill health, although not dangerous.

b. You interview others: If you appear to interview a woman on any subject, it speaks of your domestic worries. If you appear to interview a man, it speaks of jealousies and intrigues related to love and even marriage.

ISLAND. An island symbolizes your eagerness to achieve your goals singlehandedly. At the same time, depending on your situation, an island symbolizes isolation and your boredom with society.

a. You see an island: If the island appears green and is at quite a distance, it symbolizes delays in achieving your goals. But if the island appears barren, it means you are not making the required efforts. Any island near, whether green and lush or barren, means the possibilities are stronger for an earlier realization of your goals.

b. You are on an island: If the island is inhabited, it means friends or family members will ultimately rush in to help you. If there is no sign of life there, it means your goals in life are unrealistic and hence need proper planning.

IVORY. Ivory denotes prosperity and riches at the cost of others. At the same time, it denotes happiness and good health.

a. You see ivory: Ivory tusks on a live elephant signify a constructive and a modest life, whereas ivory in a shop or ivory materials on your body reflect your evil style in life, where you may perhaps live on the blood and labors of others. Seeing ivory articles on the body of others denotes an end to your unlawful ways in life through the intervention of law. Such a dream also foretells a long term of unemployment, loss, and even imprisonment through lawsuits. Touching the tusks of a live elephant, however, promises absolute prosperity, happiness, and good health.

b. You buy or sell ivory: If you buy ivory, it means you are surrounded by unscrupulous persons who will try to ruin your life. If you sell ivory, it denotes the evil continuing within you, but if you discard it, it denotes your strong will to ultimately lead a virtuous life. If you (a woman) dream of being presented with ivory materials, it denotes a successful forthcoming marriage. If already married, it signifies a happy married life.

112

J

JACKET. A jacket symbolizes protection from danger. A jacket, depending on its situation also symbolizes success in one's profession.

a. You see a jacket: Seeing one or more jackets in a shop foretells protection from a loss in business or even a financial setback through the intervention of friends. If you find yourself wearing or even holding a new jacket, it means you will very soon reach a certain stage in life where you will not only be able to care for yourself well but also for the less fortunate people. If it is an old or a torn jacket that you are either wearing or holding, it means you will continue in the same trade or profession that you presently have but with considerable success and advancement.

b. You buy or sell a jacket: Selling or buying a jacket underscores your desire to have an independent profession.

JADE. Jade is a symbol of vitality, happiness, and prosperity. This precious stone also symbolizes a return to good health for the sick and a return to normalcy for those in travail or misery.

a. You see a piece of jade: If you are sick, an early recovery is in sight. If you feel weak, you will gain vitality. If unhappy or poverty-stricken, you will receive happiness and financial gains.

b. You have the precious stone in your hands: Such a dream means fate is smiling on you, although it will not be in the form of plenty of riches. You will also have a wonderful domestic life with good children and modest riches.

JAM. Jam symbolizes a sudden and a drastic change in one's life. As such, it is not considered a good dream.

a. You see jam: If the jam appears to be dark-colored, it foretells a sudden change in your life that will not be too favorable in the long run. If it is of a light color, it suggests a search within you for an alternative to your present situation. However, the lighter the color of the jam appears in your dream, the more positive the significance appear and the changes due will bear with them a more fruitful result.

b. You buy, sell or eat jam: Buying jam suggests your boredom with life. Selling jam underscores your desire to extricate yourself from undesired company, while making jam reflects your desire to search for happiness and calm from whatever sources possible. Eating dark-colored jam indicates a strong emotional approach within you in the wake of problems, while eating light-colored jam reflects a more sagacious approach.

JESUS. Although the great Messiah's true heavenly image is not definitely known, any resemblance to his known pictures could be considered as seeing the Godly figure. His presence in one's dream has several wonderful significances. Rarely do those indulging in vice or the unrepentants dream him.

a. You see Jesus Christ: If you are a priest or a minister, it speaks of your deep attachment to spiritual values. If you are ailing, the Messiah's presence promises you a speedy and a definite recovery. If you have so far indulged in vice or crime and repent, Christ's presence in your dream will lead you to enlightenment and a virtuous life. If leading a normal life and you see Christ, you will continue to do so, but with spiritual values as a gift from seeing the Lord.

b. Jesus Christ talks to you: If Jesus appears to talk to you or even gives you his grace or affection, it is a sign that you are on the right path in life and that you should continue so. For the hopeless and the hapless and those in despair, Jesus' presence in dreams spells hope and a modest life.

JEWELRY. Jewelry symbolizes success, health, and happiness. It also symbolizes true friendship. A dream usually for women.

a. You see jewelry: If you are a businesswoman, it denotes further success in your trade. If not involved in any business, such a dream promises an early start for a beneficial future. If you are ailing, it denotes at least a partial recovery. If you have misunderstandings with your spouse and see jewelry, it foretells an early reconciliation to the satisfaction of all around you. If you have strained relations with in-laws, a favorable solution is in sight.

b. You are presented with jewelry: If your father gives you jewelry, it speaks of his continued affection and support for you. If your husband gives you jewelry, it denotes his faithful qualities. If your employer presents them to you, it foretells a promotion. If you find jewelry, it means you will alone and unaidedly climb the ladder of success.

JUDGE. A judge in one's dream has a favorable as well as unfavorable significances. Depending on the judge's situation vis-à-vis you, an interpretation can be had.

a. You see a judge: If the judge appears near you and speaks with you as a friend or an acquaintance, it means an encouragement to continue life as you presently do. It also means an appreciable success in your present occupation. But if you find yourself in the presence of a judge in his official capacity, it is a strong warning to immediately discontinue your present trends in life or face the consequences. If the judge appears to chide you or warn you, it suggests you may have committed certain acts that although not criminal, were acts least expected of you from the society. If the judge sentences you, it forebodes entanglement in legal suits. If the judge forgives you, it is a warning to be more serious and honest in your life.

b. You are a judge: To dream that you are a judge reflects the various hidden positive potentials within you that if utilized well would bring you happiness and financial gains.

JUGGLER. A juggler symbolizes artificial happiness and also symbolizes failures and indecisions of mind.

a. You see a juggler: If you know the juggler and he appears in your dream, it means you are too dependent on false hopes. If he appears juggling, it speaks of your continued failure due to your unrealistic ways of thinking.

b. You are a juggler: If you appear as a juggler, it foretells either a financial loss or problems at the place of your work. It also means you will be tempted to resort to indecent trends in life. If you appear applauded by a crowd, it foretells a failure in your present program unless you move quite fast to replan all your moves.

JUMPING. Depending on your situation and the obstacles you come across and the results, favorable as well as unfavorable results could be had.

a. You are jumping: If you appear to be jumping over an ordinary obstacle, such as a road block, a small pit, a small rock or earth formation, a fallen log or a tree branch, and successfully jump over them, it means your success whether financial, business, social or otherwise will be short-lived, since you are not making the required efforts to gain the maximum value of your ability. But if you fall or stumble while jumping, it denotes a successful fruition of your labors, thanks to your strong perseverance and objective approach to your problems. If you appear to jump from a considerable height, it is a warning to be more careful where financial matters are concerned.

b. You see others jumping: An auspicious dream foretelling a success requiring a celebration. If any person falls while jumping, it means friends will make honest efforts to extricate you from your present hardships.

JUNGLE. A dense jungle symbolizes unexpected problems, either due to negligence or due to unscrupulous business partners.

a. You see a dense jungle from a distance: This is a warning to beware of impending problems due to your indifference and negligence. Also beware of unfair business partners.

b. You are in a jungle: If you appear frightened, it means you are too perplexed or puzzled on your next step. If you appear lost, it means your past activities will bear negative results. Such a dream also warns you to refrain from getting involved in any new business venture. If you succeed in finding your way out, or even seeing tracks, it means a determined effort on your part will finally help overcome your difficulties.

K

KEEL. The keel of a ship, whether wooden or of metal, symbolizes a new beginning in life, and the end of an unhappy period.

a. You see a ship's keel: If work appears to have just begun on the keel, it is a good sign, symbolizing a new beginning. If you see a keel that has been well crafted, it means very soon you will enter a better phase in life. A damaged or an abandoned hull denotes your weakness in facing the realities of life.

b. You see an upturned keel in the water: This is an unfavorable dream, foretelling downfall and failure in life due to extravagance.

KETTLE. A kettle has favorable as well as unfavorable significances.

a. You see a kettle: An empty kettle lying on the ground or elsewhere symbolizes uncertainty to your plans and aspirations while if with water or any other liquid, it symbolizes an imminent petty quarrel that may lead to further problems. But if you see the kettle on heat or being boiled, it means that you will be able to muster courage and you could overcome your troubles. A burnt-out, misshapen, or unusable kettle means an end to tensions. If someone offers you a kettle that appears bright, polished, or a new one as a gift, it means that you will begin a new life that will compensate for your past. If you appear to throw a kettle at anyone, it means that you will have difficulties in overcoming your problems.

KEY. A key symbolizes realization of modest aspirations. For the businessman it symbolizes further prosperity.

a. You see a key: A large old key symbolizes property through inheritance. A normal key in your hands promises you the realization of your modest goals in life whether in marriage, education, or employment. Several keys in your hands symbolize the fact there are several opportunities that you can select. If you are a businessman and you dream of any of the above developments, it means further prosperity and riches through honest earnings.

b. You are given a key: Any key given to you signifies the fact that you will unexpectedly be assisted to start a good life. Finding a key suggests you will unaidedly solve your own problems. Losing a key reflects your emotional stress.

KIDNAP. To kidnap, to be kidnapped, and the act of kidnapping have various unfavorable significances.

a. You dream of a kidnapping: If you appear to witness such an act, it means that the plans you have will not bear virtuous fruits. If you happen to recognize any of the criminals, it means that you must disassociate yourself from some of your friends whom you doubt. If someone asks you to assist them in a kidnapping and you accept, it means that you will continue to have a difficult period marked by quarrels and financial problems, but if you desist or refuse, it means that very soon you will be on your way to an appreciable amelioration in life. If you find yourself participating in such an act, it means that the future appears dim and bleak unless you attach spiritual and moral values to your life. If you appear kidnapped, it means that you are attaching too much confidence to your own abilities.

KILLING. Killing someone or being killed in a dream has several significances. Presented below are several of the interpretations.

a. You kill someone: If you appear to be killing or have killed your father, it speaks of the evil intentions within you and if it's your mother, it speaks of the ungrateful character within you. If it is your brother or sister, it speaks of the jealous nature that you harbor. Killing your spouse forebodes an impending quarrel, which will cost you bitterly unless you practice calm and restraint. If someone asks you to kill a certain person and you accept, it means that you will continue to have a bad life, but if you refuse his proposal, it means that you value your future. If you ask someone to kill a person, it means that you still harbor grudge and hatred against one of your family members. Killing a beggar means that you are turning away from spiritual values while killing a friend means a lonely and a sad life for a long period. Killing a priest, a clergyman, or a nun foretells a life marked by untold miseries. Killing a policeman or a judge forebodes legal proceedings against you.

b. Someone kills you: If someone appears to be killing you, it means that you are not taking proper care of your health. It also foretells a short illness. If your brother-in-law appears to be killing you, it means conspiracies are being hatched against you, with your wife playing the leading role. It also means a divorce sooner or later. If you appear to be killed by a friend, it denotes your uncompromising nature. If you (a woman) appear to be killed by your husband, it speaks of a bitter married life. If you (a man) appear to be killed by your wife, it speaks of her unfaithfulness.

KING. A king's presence in a dream is considered to be both favorable as well as unfavorable. Depending on the king's position, several significances can be had.

a. You see a king: If the king appears friendly and relaxed, it means you will be helped by your parents. An angry king denotes impending quarrels at home. A sad king denotes a difficult period for you and the society in general. A king seated with others indicates exoneration from any accusation, while if sitting alone it speaks of a temporary period of depression and if seated on a throne symbolizes success for you in general. If a king appears to visit you or invites you, it is a sure sign of success in the latter days of your life. Seeing your king who has died means your sadness and problems will be dispelled sooner or later.

b. You are a king: A contrary dream, which forebodes unemployment and financial setbacks. If rich or prosperous and you dream you are a king, it means that you will meet with degradation and humility.

c. You give or take something from a king: Both giving as well as taking something from a king whether dead or alive, whether ruling or dethroned, is an exceptionally good sign of sudden riches and honor through your own efforts.

KISS. A kiss in a dream symbolizes happiness and an end to misunderstandings. It also symbolizes success and friendship.

a. You are kissed: If your father appears to kiss you, it speaks of his satisfaction with you. If he is dead and kisses you, it is a sign of long life. If you are ailing with a minor illness and if your dead father kisses you, it is a sign of early recovery. If your mother kisses you, it means that you are leading a normal life while if it is your siblings, it means they value your presence. If your spouse kisses you, it is a mark of respect between you. If any of your friends kiss you, it is a sign of good friendship.

b. You kiss others: Kissing your friends, business partners, or co-employees foretells a general success while kissing any of your siblings means an end to your worries. Kissing your parents indicates your grateful character. Kissing the hands of a king, a clergyman, or any holy person means that you will definitely arrive at your modest goals in life. If any of them refuse to let you kiss them, it means that you have not been living to the desired standards of society.

KITCHEN. A kitchen, depending on its situation, symbolizes several developments.

a. You see a kitchen: If the kitchen is large, clean, and with food laid on the table, it symbolizes a happy house where harmony prevails. If food is being cooked, it denotes either a satisfactory result to your labors or a visit from a friend. If your family members appear to be eating in the kitchen, it is a sign of good health. If guests appear to be eating there, it is a sign of financial prosperity or every reason for a small celebration. If you see an untidy kitchen, it means differences of opinion in the family.

b. You are in a kitchen: If you appear eating alone in a kitchen, it speaks of your desire to remain isolated while if eating with friends, it means a good project will be proposed to you soon.

KITE (a paper kite). A kite symbolizes ambitions, modesty, and even difficulties.

a. You see a kite flying: If you see the kite flying steadily at a great height, it symbolizes your high ambitions in life, which may not materialize, while if flying low, it denotes the modest nature of your plans. A kite diving towards the ground is an advice to temporarily halt new business ventures.

b. You fly a kite: If you find it easy to control the kite, it means that you will not face any difficulties in realizing your modest goals. But if you find difficulty in controlling it and the kite sways from one direction to another, it denotes an unsteady life marked by setbacks at regular intervals. A kite entangled presages several difficulties often marked by legal proceedings.

KNIFE. A knife symbolizes quarrels, arguments, illness, loss of money, and setbacks. As such, it is considered ominous in one's dream.

a. You see a knife: A small knife is a reminder to control your emotions while a large knife symbolizes quarrels within the family and even with friends.

b. You and a knife: If you appear to threaten someone with it, you will suffer from a minor illness while if you are threatened with a knife of any size, it means financial loss and even bankruptcy. However, if you appear to be using a cooking knife in the kitchen, it reflects your cautious approach to life. If you happen to buy a knife, it is a warning to control your temper at home and your place of work. A rusty knife speaks of the end of tensions and setbacks.

KNIGHT. A knight symbolizes courage, kindness, truth, and help for the less fortunate.

a. You see a knight: Seeing a knight in armor and on a steed symbolizes the courage within you to fight injustice. If the knight speaks with you in a friendly manner or even greets you, it symbolizes the absolution of any accusation. It also means an end to animosity between acquaintances. Several knights denote trustworthy friends.

b. You are a knight: A good dream reflecting your kindness. If you dream of fighting an enemy as a knight, it symbolizes your strong love for truth. It also indicates your helpful nature.

KNOT. A knot (on a string, a rope, or on a cloth) symbolizes a setback, financial loss, or perhaps a legal suit.

a. You see a knot: If it is on a string, it denotes an impending setback, perhaps financial. It can also mean quarrels within your circle of friends. On a rope it signifies a business failure and even bankruptcy. Several little knots on a string symbolize several little obstacles that could be sagaciously tackled while several of them on a rope denote the impasse that you have fallen in. If you appear to be opening the knots, it is a good sign of efforts to quickly disentangle yourself from your present problems.

b. You are tying a knot: Tying a knot on a string or rope or cloth signifies your carelessness, which will cause you problems in the future. Be wise.

L

LABORER. A laborer symbolizes ability, talent, honesty, and a contented life.

a. You see a laborer: A factory worker symbolizes hard work and ability within you. It also underscores your honesty. A farm worker signifies a productive life. A metal worker symbolizes continued good health.

b. You are a laborer: If you appear as a laborer (while not in your conscious state), it means that you are contented with whatever you have in life.

LADDER. A ladder symbolizes gains and profits. It also symbolizes success in your projects and realization of your labors.

a. You see a ladder: If the ladder appears lying on the ground, it suggests plenty of efforts have to be made in the coming days if you wish to realize your plans. If the ladder appears resting against the wall, it symbolizes your ability to achieve your goals with just a little effort.

b. You climb a ladder: Such a dream signifies an imminent success to your plans. If you appear on top of the ladder, it means that you are yet unaware of the success you have been having. If you appear to have difficulty while climbing or fall halfway, it means that you will have a short-lived setback.

LAKE. A lake symbolizes both favorable as well as unfavorable events.

a. You see a lake: A huge lake with clean and calm waters suggests an end to a long and stormy period. If the water appears dirty or unclear, it means you will continue to have a difficult period but not for long.

b. You find yourself in a lake: Swimming in the lake with calm waters denotes good health. It also means that you care much for your health.

LAMENESS. Lameness symbolizes setbacks and grief.

a. You see a lame person: If you do not recognize the person, it means you are spending too much money and time on useless projects and if you recognize the lame person, it means that a sickness will afflict one of your family members. If you see the lame person in a pitiable situation, it symbolizes a death in the family, perhaps that of a woman.

b. You see yourself as a lame person: If you see yourself lame, it is a good omen, suggesting that you will never be disgraced in life.

LAMP. A lamp symbolizes success through truth and ability. It also symbolizes a beneficial guidance.

a. You see a lamp: If the lamp appears to burn brightly, it means success through hard work and honesty. If someone appears to hold the lamp for you, it means a good friend will guide you towards a meaningful life. If you appear to be holding a lamp, it means you will unaidedly overcome your problems. If you appear to be lighting a lamp, it means very soon you will begin to seriously lay the goundworks for your future and have a new beginning.

LANDSCAPE. A landscape, depending on its description, has a favorable as well as unfavorable significances.

a. You see a landscape: A beautiful landscape with lush green fields around it foretells a happy period with a good marriage while a barren and rocky one signifies the hurdles that you will be facing in the coming days. If in business it foretells an impending loss unless you are reticent enough.

b. You find yourself in a setting: Being inside a beautiful landscape reflects your correct approach to life while being in an unattractive place reflects your irrelevance towards life in general.

LAUGHTER. Laughter in a dream symbolizes woes and hardships.

a. You laugh in a dream: This is a harbinger of a very difficult period marked by deep unhappiness. If someone is ill in the family, it is an unfortunate sign of grief, as such a dream denotes an untimely death.

b. You see others laughing: This indicates a temporary relief to your problems. But if you see your parents or siblings smiling, it is a good sign symbolizing your immediate extrication from your present situation.

LAWSUIT. Depending who files a lawsuit against you, several significances can be had.

a. A lawsuit is filed against you: If it is your spouse, it means you will have complete harmony and understanding with each other. If it is an old woman, it means you will never have any legal problems in your life while if it is an old man, it means you have to be on your guard against a person whom you doubt. If someone tells you that a lawsuit has been filed against you without revealing the name of the party, it means that the attempts by those trying to discredit you will be in vain. If you tell someone that you plan to file a suit against any person in particular, it means that you have been recently becoming too nervous.

LAWYER. A lawyer's presence symbolizes misunderstandings, fraud, jealousies, and conspiracies.

a. You see a lawyer: If the lawyer appears to be defending you, it is a sign of impending unfavorable situations due to your past mistakes. If the lawyer appears as an acquaintance and you appear to exchange a friendly conversation with him, it is a sign of impending problems within the family. If the lawyer appears unfriendly or even angry, it means you have been indulging in fraud while if he appears to counsel you, it speaks of jealousies and conspiracies against you. If you ask a lawyer to defend your case or cause and if he accepts, it means you are a victim of injustice while if he refuses, it means a lawsuit against you appears imminent although you will be the winner.

b. You are a lawyer: If you appear to be a lawyer, it means that you will properly defend yourself against bitter odds.

LEADER. A dream whose significances depend on the personality and character of the leader.

a. You see a leader: If the individual is a despot, whether living or dead, it foretells unhappy developments, perhaps a life in exile. But if the leader is or was revered and popular, it suggests promotion in work and success in business. Seeing a bad and despised leader dead or killed signifies calm after a long and a stormy period. Any leader with a gun, a sword, a hat, and threatening, suggests a terrible period marked with bloodshed, death, and destruction.

a. You are a leader: Such a dream reflects your nervousness and anger. Practice calm.

LEAVES. Leaves in one's dream symbolize good health and prosperity.

a. You see leaves: If you see green leaves on a tree, it is a good sign, which presages continued good health. If in business you will also have success. For lovers it signifies mutual understanding. Dried leaves on a tree or strewn on the ground betoken an impending quarrel with your spouse.

b. You touch leaves: If you touch green leaves on a tree, you will have a faithful love affair while touching dried leaves means failing health.

LEPROSY. Seeing a leper or appearing to have leprosy symbolizes guilt and animosity.

a. You are afflicted with leprosy: If the sight appears unbearable, it symbolizes a guilt you will have to bear for the torments and miseries you have caused others. It is suggested that a criminal usually sees such a dream. If you find yourself suddenly cured, it means that you will ultimately mend your ways.

b. You see others with leprosy: If the leper appears menacing, it suggests you have enemies pretending to be friends. If the leper speaks with you, it foretells an impending quarrel with your spouse or lover. Seeing a leper pass by indicates a temporary financial setback.

LETTER. Writing symbolizes good news, hope, and support.

a. You write a letter: Writing a letter to someone you do not identify clearly symbolizes good news and support while writing your parents indicates your love for them. A letter to your friends signifies the deep confidence you have in them. A letter to a doctor means you will recover from a minor ailment if any.

b. You receive a letter: Receiving a letter from parents means good news is on its way while letters from siblings denote support in time of need. A letter concerning employment suggests patience.

LIBRARY. A library symbolizes a lawful behavior and a realistic approach to life.

a. You see a library: If you see a library from outside, it means that your activities conform to the law of the land. If someone invites you to enter a library, it means that you will have some moral support in the coming weeks, which will greatly help you.

b. You are inside a library: Such a dream means that you are interested in uncovering the reasons of your failures if any. If inside the library someone tells you that you must read a book, it means that a certain elder within the family will soon brief you on the finer points of life, but if you find yourself sleeping in a library, it means that you are wasting time.

LIGHTHOUSE. A lighthouse in a dream symbolizes guidance, success, a fruitful and a safe journey, and a life free from legal problems.

a. You see a lighthouse: If you appear to be in a boat and you see a lighthouse, it means very soon you will have a fruitful journey. If you already have a business trip in mind, it is an assurance of success. If you find yourself looking at a brightly lighted lighthouse, it means that so far you have been getting good counselling whereas weak or dim lights warn you to reconsider your plans. If you appear to be looking out from the window of a lighthouse, it means that you will never be involved in any judicial development. An abandoned or destroyed lighthouse denotes bad companions who may be the cause of your miseries.

LIGHTNING. A favorable dream symbolizing profits, an expansion in business, recovery from illness, and an end to a bad period.

a. You see lightning: If the flash is seen in the sky, you must consider your immediate situation and position while trying to understand the significance. If you have been unemployed for more than a thousand days, you will find some form of employment and income within the next forty days if that is your most important priority at that particular moment in your conscious state. If you are ailing but not terminally, you will recover. If you are a businessman and you have been trading honestly, you can expect a good profit. If you are a writer and see the lightning strike a tree, it means that your writings will be appreciated by the society in general. If you are in the medical profession, an artist or a musician and you see the flash on any form of structure, it means your presence will be highly regarded in the society, but if you are planning any untoward act, planning to harass your spouse, extort or indulge in any form of vice or crime and you see a lightning flash either in the sky or appearing to strike at any object on earth, it means that you will finally face the law and end behind bars.

b. You see destruction by lightning: Any house, tree, or a pole destroyed by lightning means the beginning of a new cycle in life much for the better. If you appear to see your own house caught in lightning and destroyed, it signifies an end to a bad period.

LIPS. Lips in one's dream symbolize the immediate situation in life.

a. You see lips: Thin, unfriendly, and sealed lips ask you to return to the right track in life or face the consequences. Normal and friendly lips signal appreciation for the way you handle your affairs. It also means a favorable period is ahead of you. Wide-apart lips denote forthcoming problems while bleeding lips denote a quarrel with a distant family member.

b. You see your own lips: If your lips appear unhealthy or cut, it denotes an impending illness but if healthy and well-appearing, it denotes good health.

LOCK. A lock denotes safety from harm. At the same time, depending on the lock's situation, it may also symbolize an obstacle.

a. You see a lock: If the lock appears rusty and inoperable or unusable, it means that all efforts or conspiracies by enemies to block your progress are in vain. If you see a new lock, it means that you will have good protection from harm. If you try to open a lock and you appear to have difficulties, it means several obstacles have been purposely created to annoy you. With a little tact, you can overcome them. If you appear to open the lock easily, it means that you will neutralize or frustrate their efforts. Breaking a lock reflects your unfair means in life.

b. You use a lock: If you appear to lock any precious item in a safe, it means that you will have safety while locking any human being in a room or any other place betokens a legal procedure against you.

LOCOMOTIVE. A locomotive symbolizes determination, prosperity, and happiness.

a. You see a locomotive: If the locomotive appears to speed by, it denotes happy days are finally arriving. If the locomotive is stationary, it reflects your determination to gain prosperity through honest means. If you appear to walk towards the locomotive, it means very soon you will have a short journey that will greatly influence your future. A derailed locomotive warns you to be more realistic in life.

LOVE. Falling in love in one's dream symbolizes loneliness and a strong desire to have a companion.

a. You fall in love: If you appear to fall in love with a person whom you know, the chances are that you will never speak with that person. If unmarried, it reflects your loneliness. If you happen to fall in love with a person whom you do not know, it means that very soon you will meet an interesting person with whom you will develop a friendly relation but one that will not last long.

b. You fall in love with a former friend: If married and you dream so, it reflects the deep love you still have for that person.

LUGGAGE. Luggage in any form in a dream symbolizes separation, divorce, breakage in friendship, and homelessness.

a. You see luggage: Such a dream means to beware of your behavior, relations and dealings with friends and business partners or with people at your place of work. If you see someone carrying his luggage, it warns of the consequences of quarrels you may get involved in. Seeing your spouse going away with his luggage symbolizes a divorce or separation, while if you yourself go away with luggage, that means homelessness.

M

MADMAN. A madman has both favorable as well as unfavorable significances. Depending on your position vis-à-vis the madman's, an interpretation can be had. A madwoman has no significance.

a. You see a madman: If the madman appears friendly, it is a good sign, indicating a valuable new friendship. If he gives you any good news, it is a sign of encouragement, but if he gives you some disheartening news, it is a direct prophecy of legal problems awaiting you. If he approaches you menacingly, it means you have to begin acting in order to gain a place in society. It also underscores your lazy nature. If the madman appears to shout or cry uncontrollably, it is a direct warning to beware of your risky adventures whose consequences will not be to your favor. If the madman gives you a gift of something, it suggests a future help from someone you least expected. Quarreling with a madman reflects your nervous attitude. Giving him something reflects your ability to stand on your own feet.

b. You are a madman: This is a dream said to be chiefly for those passionately in love. Beware of temptations and meditate.

MAN. Depending on the man's description and position, an interpretation both favorable as well as otherwise can be had.

a. You see a man: If you (a man) see a well-dressed and a well-figured man, it suggests you will have a normal life. If the man appears abnormally huge but not a giant, it reflects your high ambitions that require an alteration. If you see a man whom you know but he appears as a dwarf in your dreams, it means you are underestimating your own potentials. If it is a man you know who appears naked, it spells prosperity, while if it is a man you know who appears dead, it means a long and a healthy life for you. Any male friend who

130

appears naked means that you should disassociate yourself from him.

MARBLE. This stone symbolizes extravagance, prosperity, loss, and quarrels.

a. You see marble: If it is a large chunk of uncut marble, it symbolizes prosperity but only with a cautious approach and a logical outlook. If you see blocks of cut marble, it symbolizes your excesses in life, perhaps extravagance coupled with folly. If you appear to see cracks in them, it symbolizes a future loss in business. If you appear to pick up a piece, it means that you will make a desperate attempt to avert the problems that you are presently undergoing, which are the consequences of your own mistakes.

b. You buy or sell marble: Buying marble foretells an end to financial problems while selling it spells the beginning of quarrels within the family. Working with marble slabs on a construction site signifies your voracious behavior.

MARKET. A marketplace symbolizes plenty, a good married life, good health, and friendly relations with all.

a. You see a market either from far or near: Seeing a market full of eatables and other utilities signifies plenty, in the sense that you will never experience a dearth of your basic needs in life. If you see a huge crowd there, it denotes a modest purchasing power in you.

b. You are in a market: If you appear in a market alone, it signifies your egoistic behavior while if with friends or family members, it denotes harmony with those around you and in the family. Buying anything there signifies your good health. If you find yourself alone in the market with nobody in sight, it means that you are taking too many risks in business and financial affairs.

MARRIAGE. Marriage in a dream has several significances, favorable as well as otherwise.

a. You and a marriage: If you are unmarried and dream of someone else's marriage, it underscores the deep anguish and unhappiness within you. If you dream of marrying a person whom you "one-sidedly love," it means that you will never marry that person, much to your own benefit. If you are married and dream again of your marriage ceremony, it signals shaky relations with your spouse. It may also mean a divorce in the future. If you happen to witness any commotion in a marriage, it connotes domestic problems for you only if you are married. If unmarried, it means quarrels with your friends.

MASK. A mask symbolizes falsehood, slyness, fraud, and cheating. It is also a symbol of bad days in later days in life.

a. You see a mask: Any form of mask but not worn by anyone means an early warning to amend your ways in life or face the consequences. Several of them signify impending legal problems arising out of your past fraudulent activities. If you appear to see yourself with a mask, it means that you are a sly cheat. If you (a man) see your wife with a mask, it is a direct signal to get rid of her presence in a legal manner and if you (a woman) see your husband with a mask, it means that he no longer can be trusted as being honorable. It also means that your husband will soon get entangled in legal problems that will finally put him behind bars.

MEAT. Meat, depending on its situation, has several significances, favorable as well as unfavorable.

a. You see meat: Huge chunks of meat are a sign of a favorable financial deal while small pieces mean a modest gain. Cooked meat denotes the continuation of good health while meat thrown away or lying on the ground forebodes a short illness.

b. You are eating meat: If you appear to be eating meat in nominal amount, it means you enjoy a balanced mind while if you appear to be devouring or eating a lot of it or if there are large quantities of cooked meat on your plate, it underscores your easily agitated behavior. It also foretells disagreements ending in quarrels.

c. You buy or sell meat: Buying meat denotes guests whom you consider dependable while selling meat denotes friendly relations with all.

MEDAL. Medals in one's dream symbolize respect, truth, success, and honor.

a. You appear with medals: A good dream presaging good times ahead of you. If leading a normal life, it means success at work, at business and financial matters. If running for an office, it spells success through the confidence and respect the society has for you. If in the armed forces, it speaks of your exemplary courage and discipline. It also signifies your fiercely truthful nature.

b. You see others with medals: If you know the person bedecked with medals, it underscores your admiration for truth and modesty and if you do not recognize the person, it means you will have thoughtful and dependable friends.

MEDICINE. Medicine in a bottle or in any other form of packing symbolizes illness and unhappiness.

a. You see medicine: In any packing, medicine warns you to take professional care of your health. It also asks you to refrain from using any intoxicant. If there are several bottles or packings of medicine lying around you, it forebodes a death in the family. If someone asks you take medicine, it means that you will have a short period of unhappiness.

MILK. Milk is a sign of joy and fortunate developments.

a. You see milk: Milk in a bottle, can, or glass signifies joy within you. Spilt milk denotes the indecisiveness and timidity within you.

b. You drink, buy, or sell milk: Drinking milk signifies a robust health. If you are ill and you dream so, it means a partial recovery is in sight. Buying milk denotes your wish to abhor vice while selling milk reflects your visions of a modest life. Throwing away milk means you are undecided on your next move. Concentrate through prayers and meditation.

MINE. A mine symbolizes loss, hardships, and dangers.

a. You see a mine: A functioning mine with miners working indicates hardships will afflict you unless you move fast enough to rectify your errors. Entering a mine warns you to eschew undesired friends who may ruin you through false promises. An abandoned mine warns you of dangers haunting you. If you see or someone tells you of miners trapped inside the shafts, it means that you have to use your wisdom and sense to extricate yourself from your present problems.

b. You are a miner: Being a miner in your dream reflects your illogical means that could cause you financial and domestic problems. But if in the conscious state, you are a miner and dream of working in the mines, it underscores your truthful and honest means in life.

MIRROR. A mirror is a reminder of your goodness and helpful ways in life. Rarely does one with a notorious character see a mirror in a dream. Strangely enough, in rare instances does one see himself or herself in a mirror.

a. You see a mirror: If you see a mirror, it is a sign of gratitude from those around you for the services and help you have rendered them. If the mirror is small, it means that you are aware that your humanitarian mission is not yet over. A cracked mirror reminds you not to concede to sinful temptations.

b. You are presented a mirror: Whether large or small, decorated or simple, a mirror received as a gift signifies the love of the society for you. It also means that your survivors will arrive at a stage of perfection where they too will dedicate themselves to the cause of the unfortunates.

MONEY. Depending on the position of the money and the amount, several significances can be had.

a. You see money: If you dream of seeing money strewn all around you, it signifies a sudden breakthrough in your luck, mostly for the better. If you appear to pick up the money (only if in a modest amount), it presages a good gift, perhaps in cash from a friend. If you appear to see a few notes here and there, it means that you will have an appreciable amount with you in the next few weeks.

b. You are given money: If you receive money from your parents, it signifies their support for you; if from a girlfriend, it means a false love; and if you receive it from your boyfriend, it means you are a fraud. If you receive money from your spouse, it means that there is a complete accord on developments within the family. If you receive money from a beggar, it means you will have a difficult period marked by unbearable hardships. If you receive money from a person whom you identify as being rich, it means you will be soon proposed with a fruitful business venture. If your employer gives you money, it means a successful career. If any of your children give you money, it means you will never be in need.

MOON. A moon symbolizes honesty, true love, hope, and tranquillity within the family. It also symbolizes health recovery.

a. You see the moon: A full moon in all its glory underscores your absolute honesty in life. It also symbolizes happiness and recovery from minor illness. It also presages an end to misunderstandings between friends and in the family. A half-moon indicates your undecided nature whereas a crescent underlines your values for a spiritual life.

b. You feel you are very near to the moon: Such a dream presages a prosperous life. It also means that you will never know poverty.

MOTHER. A mother in one's dream is exceptionally favorable. Her presence symbolizes moral and spiritual support with healing.

a. You see your mother: If you are unhappy and you see your mother, her presence presages a gradual end to unhappiness. If sick, you will recover at least partially. If alone, forsaken, or isolated by the society, you will have better days.

b. You receive something from your mother: A wonderful dream signifying protection from any evil temptations and even harm. If you give something to your mother, it denotes a prosperous life with a dignified profession.

MOUNTAIN. A mountain symbolizes both favorable as well as unfavorable significances.

a. You see a mountain: Such a dream means that you are underestimating your abilities and talents. With a little encouragement, you will be able to overcome this feeling and realize your goals. If you appear to see a mountain in a place that did not exist before, it means obstinate obstacles will challenge you. Solve your problems, if any, with wisdom and care.

b. You are on the summit of the mountain: A wonderful reminder that you are near your goals in life. Falling from a mountain while climbing reflects your fickle and hasty nature.

MOURNING. Contrary to what it implies, mourning in one's dream symbolizes good luck, a new beginning in life, and a modest life.

a. You see people mourning: If you recognize any person mourning, it suggests good luck and if you do not, it means that you are on the right track of life where you must continue to work hard towards your goals. If you see any of your family members mourning, it means that you will soon have a new beginning in life that will ultimately bring forth with it a modest life coupled with happiness.

b. You are mourning: Such a dream suggests great potential within you that if utilized properly will benefit you much.

MOUTH. A mouth symbolizes greed, fickle nature, and quarrels.

a. You see a mouth: A wide-opened mouth denotes the greed and quarrelsome nature within you. A closed mouth reflects your unpredictable and duplicitous nature. A normal and a pleasant-appearing mouth symbolizes prosperity and friendly relations with all. It also reflects good health. A bleeding mouth denotes a lawsuit.

b. You see your own mouth: If laughing, it denotes that you have committed an unlawful act. If you appear to be crying, it means an end to domestic worries. It also means a compromise with your spouse if sharing any misunderstanding.

N

NAIL. Hammering nails or just seeing them symbolizes problems that have to be sorted out with sagacity.

a. You see nails: If you see a single nail, it suggests a forthcoming dispute with your employer (if employed) or a dispute with your business partner (if in business) or a temporary setback (if self-employed) and unemployment (if yet unemployed) at least for the foreseeable future. A heap of them suggests your perplexity in finding a solution to your plight.

b. You are hammering a nail: If you appear driving a nail into a door, it suggests you are unwittingly blocking your own path to progress. If using a nail on a box, it betokens quarrels with your close family members. However, drawing out nails from a door or any other wooden object foretells a new beginning for the better but with much delay.

NATIVE COUNTRY. This dream has significance only for those who do not reside in their native country. One's native country symbolizes an absolutely new life with better friends.

a. You dream you are suddenly in your native country: If you are residing abroad and you suddenly find yourself in the streets of the city of your native country or your village, it foretells a sudden development in your life that you will greatly appreciate. This means new employment opportunities, new friends, and perhaps a new address, all for the better. If you desire to leave or escape your native country to which you have returned in your dream and you find it difficult, it means you are less responsible for the problems facing you. But if there is no difficulty to do so, it means you will mend your relations with your spouse (if estranged) or with your friends if there was any misunderstanding.

NECKLACE. A necklace symbolizes prosperity, riches, and happiness.

a. You see a necklace: If worn by a woman you recognize, your sister, your mother, or your spouse, it foretells a sudden breakthrough in your business and your life in general. If you do not recognize the person wearing the necklace, it presages a business offer where you will benefit. If you see a necklace in a shop, on a table, or elsewhere, but not fallen on the floor, it denotes a general contentment in life. If someone asks you to steal a necklace or if you are in the act of committing such a crime, it means that no matter how well placed you are, you will yet indulge in fraud.

b. You buy a necklace: If you appear to buy a necklace without arguing the price, it means a financial gain but indulging in arguments presages difficulties due to your obstinate behavior. Receiving a necklace as a gift is a direct prophecy of getting a worthy gift from a person you know. Finding a necklace speaks of exceptional friends. Losing or searching for your necklace reflects your reckless behavior.

NEEDLES. Needles symbolize favorable as well as unfavorable developments.

a. You see needles: A heap of needles foretells impending arguments, chiefly matrimonial, often ending in an ugly scene. A single needle foretells lawsuits against you by an elderly woman. If you happen to hold a needle in your hand, it reflects your determination to tactfully confront your foes. If you prick someone with it, a great deal of nervousness still exists within you.

b. You thread a needle: Threading a needle suggests you will eventually tackle your woes much to your own satisfaction. Holding a threaded needle reflects your readiness to embark on a new life.

NEST. A nest, depending on its situation, has favorable as well as unfavorable significances.

a. You see a nest: If it is a big nest with eggs or the young ones in it but without the mother bird in sight, it speaks of your ability to live a modest life without depending on others. The mother's presence, however, means that you should think well in advance before you embark on any new plans. An empty nest, whether small or large, betokens unhappy days.

b. You rob or destroy a nest: A bad sign reflecting your ruthless behavior. It also means endless sufferings due to your criminal past and present. Killing the young ones, stealing the eggs, or destroying them means a sickness in the family that could result in the death of a young one. Killing the mother bird or even attempting to kill it forebodes a terrible illness for your spouse. But trying to build a nest for the birds means a spiritual gain. If you come across a destroyed nest, it means your recklessness will eventually cost you your happiness.

NET. A net symbolizes difficulties, though not major. A net in a dream reminds one to be serious in life.

a. You see a net: A net for fishing, trapping birds, or for other purposes serves as a reminder to be more practical and realistic or face the consequences, which although not severe will greatly hamper your progress.

b. You appear entangled in a net: A serious warning to desist from your emotional and angry temperaments, especially in relations with your friends. It also foretells a legal suit if you continue to behave so. If you manage to free yourself from the net, it means you will gradually mend your ways and have better times.

NOSE. A nose, depending on its shape and situation, has several significances both favorable as well as otherwise.

a. You see a nose: "Only if you see well," a small and a funny-looking nose denotes petty quarrels through jealousy. A large one denotes harmony at home. A large nose also predicts an appreciable financial gain. A bulbous nose reflects your friendly and helpful attitude while a hawked nose underscores your miserly behavior. A bleeding nose forebodes humiliation in love. It also means a broken promise.

NUDITY. Seeing others or yourself nude symbolizes a hard period coupled with acute unhappiness and poverty.

a. You find yourself nude: If you find yourself nude and in a poor quarter of the city, it foretells a period marked by unemployment, unhappiness, and even poverty. If you manage to find a cloth or some clothing to cover yourself, it means the problems will be temporary. But if you find yourself either in a posh part of the city, a village, or even the countryside in this situation, it means there are several possibilities for you to develop your life, but you are not making the required efforts. Sleeping in the nude means evil acquaintances. Sleeping in the nude but with a blanket over you on the pavements of a street underscores the terrible period you are undergoing, but there is no need to worry, since things will suddenly change much to your surprise.

b. You see others in the nude: If you see your parents naked, it means you have not performed your obligations towards them. If it is your brother or sister, it means that you have been unfair to them. If you see any of your friends in such a situation, it means that you must disassociate yourself from any of them whom you suspect.

NUMBERS. Among the "masters" with whom several sessions of discussions concerning the significances of the presence of numbers or figures in one's dream were held, four of them, Hamid Ibn Qader, Muhammad Ibn Rasool, Jassem Ibn Sarraf, and Hakim Burhan Beig, dismissed their values as insignificant and maintained their reservations about them in a dream. Nevertheless, the majority of the masters viewed numbers in a dream as having some significant significance. The four claimed that numbers in a dream are manifested chiefly due to emotional factors, such as the number of days of agony, expectation of a favor, a help, a certain period to accomplish a certain act, debts, amount of goods to be sold or bought and likewise. How do we recognize or identify if at all NUMBERS? Various signs go to assist us. The figures may appear in various forms. On a tree, on a wall, on clothes, on a vehicle, or any other object. It may be in the form of one or more figures. Someone may suggest or call out a figure or may write it. You may yourself write it. We may even murmur it to ourselves. If the numbers appear in compound form, they are to be simplified or reduced to a single number not exceeding nine by adding the figures till you arrive at one single figure. An example would be a complex figure such as 849, which when reduced would be $8 + 4 + 9 = 21 = 2 + 1 = 3$. An important point while interpreting numbers in your dream is that you must impartially consider your immediate situation.

ONE: This figure symbolizes success, loneliness, profit, and even loss. If you have a specific profession, you may expect an agreeable degree of success. If you are unemployed, you may expect at least a modest offer. If you have recently separated from your spouse or your beloved, it is a sign of loneliness for the foreseeable future. If you have recently had any argument with any of your friends, it means it is doubtful that the relations will ever heal again. If you have recently purchased any object or thing solely to sell it later, you may expect a small profit, but if you have a partner in buying and selling goods and if you see the figure one, a loss is to be expected.

TWO: This figure symbolizes disagreements, arguments, and obstacles. If planning to intercede on any person's behalf, caution is advocated. If desiring to solve any family disputes, such a figure in a dream tells you that now is not the right time. If planning to negotiate a business deal, postpone it for at least one week. It is also advisable not to attend any family gatherings if you feel depressed, bear animosity towards any one of them, or intend to enter into any arguments, since it will create bad relations for the future.

THREE: This number suggests friendship and good health. If you have strained relations with acquaintances, there are hopes for an early reconciliation. There are also chances to meet a new friend. If someone appears to write this figure in front of you or write it over your clothes, it means a sudden and a costly gift is on its way. If you happen to murmur it or reflect it to someone, it indicates within the next three days or at the most three weeks you will arrive at one of your modest desires. If ailing with minor illness, a recovery is not far away.

FOUR: A propitious figure symbolizes stability, security, and the realization of modest projects. This figure is said to bring good luck to the farmer in particular. If expecting any form of returns for your labors, a good return is assured. If awaiting the realization of your modest projects (maturing of crops and farm products for the farmer), there is every indication that it will be realized. If intending to make modest purchases for future business reasons, the gains will, although not high, be quite appreciable.

FIVE: This figure, if seen, greatly assists one to understand the various reasons for continued setbacks. It has been suggested that usually a person trying hard to gain information about the identity of his tormentors gets a faint glimpse of the identity of that person after the figure gets manifested or chanted in his dream. If you are unawaredly at fault for your own setbacks, you will realize it. This would be in the form of your repeatedly calling out either four days, four objects, four persons, or four other things. If others appear to be guilty for your woes, you will either see the figure, others will pronounce it in some form or the other or will appear to write it on any surface. If someone appears to be "writing" this figure with a pointed stick or object on soft ground, it means that someone had been or has been futilely planning your destruction. But there is no reason to be disheartened, since the planners of doom for you will themselves disappear before they could harm you.

SIX: This figure chiefly deals with developments within the family. If you have misunderstandings with your parents, you may expect a sudden change of heart to the satisfaction of all. For those married and experiencing an uneasy period, such a figure in dream promises a change for the better. Siblings separated for a long period can expect an accidental reunion. For cousins separated such a dream means a reunion is ruled out, at least for the foreseeable future. If absolutely alone and you see such a figure in your dream, it means, if you pay a short visit to any one of your nearest family members, there are all indications that it will be very beneficial, to your surprise.

SEVEN: This figure symbolizes delight and satisfaction to the extent of necessitating a celebration. If you have been experiencing a lengthy period of hardships either in the form of financial or social difficulties, a good degree of amelioration is presaged. If you have recently appeared in any examination, the results will be to your desire. If you are expecting an answer to your requests, the answer will be to your satisfaction. If you have recently clinched a business deal, the results will greatly satisfy you. For those separated a sudden reunion is possible. But this dream also spells loss and problems for gamblers and financial speculators. For those in despair and hopeless, such a figure in a dream spells a partial end to their problems.

EIGHT: This figure chiefly deals with financial activities. If unemployed and if you have been making honest efforts to seek employment, a good hope is foreseen anytime within the next forty days. If experiencing acute financial problems, a modest amelioration through the intervention of a "long lost friend" is presaged. If expecting to receive back an amount owed to you, there is a possibility that you will recover at least half of it very soon.

NINE: This figure symbolizes uncertainty, loss and ill health. If you are planning to invest, enter into any business negotiation, buy or sell any property, this figure reminds you to refrain from doing so for at least a fortnight. If planning to intervene in any family affair, it is better to do so at a much later date. If planning a long journey, postpone it to the next week, but if planning to undertake a short journey not exceeding sunrise to sunset and definitely returning to your place of residence before it, there is no harm foreseen. If ailing, desist from indulging in any act that may aggravate your health.

NUN. A nun symbolizes truth, modesty, comfort, spiritual values, and happiness. It also signifies good health and a successful business opportunity.

a. You see a nun: If the nun passes you, it foretells a happy reunion of friends and the elimination of animosity between family members if any. If she makes a friendly gesture, it is an encouragement to uphold truth in life. If the nun converses with you, it means that one day you will seek spiritual values. If you ask her any question and she answers you, it presages a good business. If she refuses to answer you, it means you must refrain from entering into any commercial

143

activity at least for the next forty days. Quarreling with a nun betokens unhappy days.

b. You give something to the nun: Giving a nun something reflects your absolute satisfaction for your achievements while receiving something from her indicates exceptional health. If you are ailing, the nun's gifts symbolize a cure.

NURSE. A nurse symbolizes help and a modest financial situation.

a. You see a nurse: A nurse at work symbolizes help for you, which could greatly enhance your living standard. A nurse telling you that you will recover (if you are ailing) means that your life is not in imminent danger and if not ailing but having other difficulties whether social or financial, they will be gradually solved, although not fully. If the nurse tells you that you appear in bad health while you enjoy good health, it means that there are chances that you may fall on bad days due to your own faults. If she describes your robust health or praises you, it means much has to be done to maintain the minimum required in life.

b. You are a nurse: Such a dream foretells an advantageous business deal that would fulfill your modest financial requirements. If you find yourself treating others, it foretells domestic happiness.

O

OAR. Oars in one's dream symbolize possibilities and success. At the same time depending on other situations, they signify unhappiness and loss.

a. You see oars: Just seeing a pair of them means assistance from friends can be expected in time of need while a single one denotes a friendly advice will save you in case you heed them. One or more of them in your hands signify a correct start in life while if you see someone else holding them, it means that you have not been giving sufficient priority to your projects. Broken oars forebodes petty obstacles in your daily affairs while intentionally breaking them or throwing them away means you are becoming restless and to an extent undependable. Receiving them from someone denotes good chances in life.

b. You use oars: If you happen to use them well, it foretells a good fortune coupled with a good future while having difficulty using one or two of them or losing them over the side means quarrels, bad news, illness, and even disappointment in love.

OASIS. An oasis symbolizes sanctuary and relief. Depending on the situation, it also symbolizes loss and misunderstanding.

a. You see an oasis: If you appear to see the oasis either from far or near, it signifies sanctuary from miseries and problems, thanks to dependable friends. If you find yourself inside an oasis, it is a sign of relief from continued family feuds. If you are in business, it means continued prosperity. If the oasis turns out to be a mirage, and if you think so, negative values substitute the above statements, in the sense that misunderstandings, loss, and unhappiness will increase for you.

b. You see others in an oasis: Seeing others in an oasis means that you are learning well the secrets to find fame while if you see any quarrel there, it means that things will not eventually be in your favor while if you see any celebrations over there, it is a sure sign of success for your past labors.

OCEAN. An ocean, depending on its situation, symbolizes good health, wealth, and friendly relations with all.

a. You see an ocean: If the ocean is calm and clear, it symbolizes a success in love, probably with a person older than you. If you see a ship or any vessel from far or near, it foretells that very soon you will have enough wealth and fortune either through business, inheritance, or simply speaking, vast sums from a well-wisher. If you find yourself very much near the ocean, it presages an excellent health, although not a long life. A stormy ocean asks you to be cautious in each and every step you take.

b. You swim in an ocean: A dream suggesting your desire to conquer impossible obstacles and to do the impossible. Be sagacious and practice restraint where your emotions are concerned. If you appear to be drowning in the ocean or you appear very frightened, you must consider the dream as organic without any significance. If you appear to be helping someone caught in a stormy ocean, it means that you desire friendly relations with one and all.

OINTMENT. Any ointment in one's dream symbolizes cure, a modest life, and a helping character.

a. You see ointment: Whether in a metal or glass covering, it foretells an imminent cure for minor ailments. If you appear to use the ointment, it is a direct warning to take care of your health.

OLD AGE/OLD PERSON. Old age, true to its name, symbolizes a long and a healthy life.

a. You see yourself as an old person: For a woman of any age, it foretells the surprises of a youthful appearance, even in old age. For a man it foretells a calm life coupled with a long life. If you are young (below twenty) and you dream about your youthfulness, it means that you will have a life full of hurdles where it will be necessary for you to make certain sacrifices to reach your goals. But if sick, it presages a recovery even if partial.

b. You see yourself among old persons: If you are young and have such a dream, it means a life free from lawsuits. If you are old and a person tells you that you look young, it means that certain persons are conspiring against you. If you are young and you appear to exchange a pleasant conversation with old persons, it means success through hard labor.

OPIUM. Opium in any form or situation in a dream symbolizes misery, loss, illness, and misunderstandings. It also symbolizes a divorce and even a loss of life.

a. You see opium: Just seeing opium in any form means a strong warning to immediately stop indulging in illegal acts. It also warns of impending miseries if you do not hasten to mend your ways. If you happen to touch opium, it betokens disgrace and dishonor.

b. You smoke or utilize opium: An extremely unfavorable dream, foretelling financial loss leading to bankruptcy and coupled with illness from which you may not recover. Others seen using opium is a strong warning to beware of bad friends.

ORPHANS. An orphan symbolizes happiness as well as unhappiness in one's life.

a. You see an orphan: If you know the orphan and if he appears happy, it denotes a continued good period both in domestic and financial affairs, but if he appears unhappy and grieving, it foretells a rough period ahead of you. If someone tells you that the child you are looking at is an orphan, it signifies a divorce if you are married or a temporary separation if engaged. If you appear to give affection to the orphan, it foretells the prospects of a good marriage.

b. You are an orphan: If you dream of being an orphan, it means that you have not been utilizing your talents and abilities in the right direction.

P

PAIN. Any form of pain in a dream symbolizes a temporary setback in general affairs. If you have fever or illness and dream of pain, it is an organic dream without any prophetic significance.

a. You feel pain: If your muscles ache in general, you will have some argument with your spouse or lover and also at work. Pain in the ears denotes your unwillingness to accept constructive criticisms. Pain in the eyes reflects your unpreparedness to face the challenges in life.

b. You see somebody in pain: A warning to take great care in your everyday affairs. If it is any family member, it foretells anguish due to an accident.

PAINTER. A painter symbolizes the ability to do things, encouragement, and the realization of a project.

a. You see a painter: A painter at work symbolizes your abilities and talents to get work done. A painter who appears to have just finished his work is a symbol of encouragement to continue your quest in life. If the painter speaks to you, it foretells the realization of a goal but with patience.

b. You are a painter: A significant dream suggesting you will arrive at your goals only if you make a continued and a serious effort.

PALACE. A palace symbolizes tyranny and falsehood. At the same time, depending on the situation of the palace, it also has a favorable significance.

a. You see a palace: Just seeing a palace from far away underscores your tyrannical behavior, while near, it warns you to beware of undependable and false acquaintances who surround you for ulterior motives. Entering an empty palace signifies false promises from ruthless persons whose only aims are to utilize your presence. If the palace appears to be full of people, it symbolizes generous help from a friend. If you happen to see a head of state or a king or even a prince to whom the palace is related, it marks the beginning of a fruitful life, thanks to your own honest efforts.

PASSPORT. A passport symbolizes success of your plans in life, whether in business or romance.

a. You see a passport: Just seeing a passport, even if it is not yours, is a signal to go ahead with your projects. If you see your own passport, it is a good sign foretelling a beneficial trip.

b. You and a passport: Applying for a passport means there are signs indicating success in your business or at your place of work. If you are handed over your passport by an official, it foretells an imminent profit or a promotion. Having a passport in your hand or with you promises a beautiful surprise within the next few months, which will be very much to your benefit and liking. Being refused a passport means you will have to replan and think over your next move. Misplacing, forgetting, or temporarily losing your passport denotes flaws and irregularities in your plans. If your passport appears to be impounded, it is a warning to stay away from trouble and take great care of your day-to-day affairs, since it means an impending legal procedure against you.

PEARL. Pearls symbolize a good health, riches through inheritance, and success in business and at work. It also symbolizes an exceptionally good marriage together with friendly relations with all.

a. You see pearls: If you see a single pearl, it denotes exceptionally good health. If it is on a string or chain, it means you will meet a good love partner. If you appear to be wearing it, it foretells a gift from a friend or admirer. If you see several pearls, it is a sign of riches through inheritance. If the pearls appear stringed or on a chain, it speaks of your ability to have a successful business. If you appear to wear them, success in business is imminent.

b. You present pearls to your lover: Presenting pearls to the one you love means you will have a good marriage while to your spouse it is a symbol of a happy married life.

c. You receive pearls: Receiving one or more pearls from any person reflects the good relations you have with all.

d. You buy or sell pearls: Buying pearls either foretells a sudden financial loss or a breakup with your business partners while selling pearls suggests you are experiencing financial difficulties at the moment.

PHARMACY. A pharmacy symbolizes illness, disputes, and unhappiness at home.

a. You see a pharmacy: Just seeing a pharmacy whether at near or from a distance foretells an impending illness that may continue for some time.

b. You are inside a pharmacy: Being inside a pharmacy means you

149

will have heated disputes with your family members and even your spouse that will result in a bitter unhappiness at home. You will also suffer from illness. Buying medicine in a pharmacy denotes you will eventually find a suitable solution to your unhappiness at home and even partially recover your health, while leaving the pharmacy empty-handed suggests you will be faced with your problem at least for the foreseeable future.

PICTURES. Pictures symbolize the existence of conspiracies and slanders unknown to a person. Depending on the position of the pictures vis-à-vis you, an interpretation reflecting the eventual unearthing of the conspiracies could be had.

a. You see pictures: A single picture reflects a few current problems as a result of conspiracies and slanders while several pictures denote a host of problems.

b. You are presented a picture: A significant dream foretelling the discovery of the reasons for failure afflicting you, through the help of an acquaintance. If several pictures are presented to you, it suggests several persons will assist you in unearthing and neutralizing slanders spread against one.

c. You buy or sell pictures: Buying or selling pictures reflects your inner desire for a constructive and a positive approach to life devoid of slandering or defaming others or indulging in vice of any sort.

PILGRIMAGE. Going on a pilgrimage denotes good luck, happiness, good health, and continued success in your work and profession. A pilgrimage also underscores the truth within you and the importance you attach to spiritual values.

a. You are going on a pilgrimage: Beginning a journey on a pilgrimage suggests good luck in the forthcoming months. If alone, it suggests you will have to be wise enough in utilizing the good chances offered you. If with others, it means you will have wise counsel from friends and supporters. If you appear to be near the holy shrine, it suggests happiness at home, good health, and continued success in your trade.

b. You are inside the shrine: Such a dream foretells success in arriving at your goals. At the same time, it underscores the values you attach to truth, modesty, and spiritual values.

PIRATE. A pirate symbolizes dangerous adventures, temptations, risks, and an unsteady life.

a. You see a pirate: If the pirate appears on a ship (just as in the old), it denotes you are about to unguardedly, or rather are made to embark on strange adventures and risks, which would not be to your benefit in the long run. Refrain from such acts and seek professional help. If the pirate appears on land, it is a strong warning to select the right friends and desist from temptations.

b. You are a pirate: Such a dream underscores the fact that you have already entered an undesirable phase in your life that will sway you away from a normal life and place your career in jeopardy. If you dream of attacking someone with your group, it foretells an unhappy future with lawsuits against you.

PLOUGHING. Ploughing symbolizes a person's desire to remain traditional with a virtuous life. It also symbolizes a good married life and modest fortunes.

a. You see a plough: Such a dream strengthens your desire to remain traditional with spiritual values and a virtuous life.

b. You are ploughing: If you appear ploughing alone, it is a good dream, indicating a good fortune through your own efforts. If you are being assisted by someone, it means you will be helped by your relatives in case you so desire. If you appear to have just finished ploughing, you can expect to have a dignified and a modest life with average holdings.

c. You see others ploughing: If you see others ploughing, it means you will have a good and a helpful spouse.

POISON. Poison in a dream symbolizes a bad ending to relations, misunderstandings in the family, separation, divorce, and even a loss of life.

a. You see poison: Poison in any form foretells quarrels with friends often ending in violence. If you hold it in your hand, it foretells violent arguments with your spouse, ending in separation or even a divorce. If someone appears to consume poison, it is a strong warning to refrain from any untoward action. If you continue, it may end in a loss of life.

b. You consume poison: Such a dream underscores your suicidal tendency. Practice meditation, regularly visit a place of worship, and seek professional counsel.

POLICEMAN. A policeman symbolizes help, consolation, truth, and modest gains.

a. You see a policeman: If the policeman proposes to help or guide you, it denotes help from all friends and acquaintances and a green light to go ahead. If you are planning to embark on a business venture, now is the time, since all possibilities appear in your favor. If you are unemployed, you will find the right work. If unhappy you will find consolation. If you argue with a policeman, it means you have to straighten up your situation vis-à-vis those concerned with you.

b. You are a policeman: Such a dream underscores your desire to uphold truth and the law. It also foretells a modest-to-average life, depending on your desires.

POLYANDRY—POLYGAMY. Polyandry or polygamy, if practiced or even discussed in a dream, symbolizes miseries and misfortunes. As such, it is considered one of the most unfavorable dreams a person could ever have.

a. You commit polyandry or polygamy: Such a dream forebodes quarrels, arguments, and continued bickerings at home if you are married. It also denotes terrible misunderstandings between you and your spouse that could end in divorce. If unmarried but engaged, it means a permanent separation. Those having such dreams and not practicing such an immoral and an unspiritual act are admonished restraint and control of their emotions through prayers and visit to a place of worship.

b. You are tempted to commit or indulge in such an act: Just being tempted means you are quite weak in making the right and timely decisions. Just a little more effort and you will fall on the right track. If you appear to discuss such a malicious act, it means you are knowingly taking yourself to the brink of abyss with consequences you will deeply regret.

PORTER. A porter symbolizes hardships, financial problems, and even ill health.

a. You see a porter: A porter carrying a load foretells hardships due to a financial loss or a business failure. It also suggests problems at work, possibly ending in dismissal. A porter standing or sitting idly foretells a long period of idleness.

b. You are a porter: If you dream you are a porter, it suggests you are confused as to what next step you should take in life. If someone offers you luggage or a load, it means you will be assisted to lead a normal life.

PRAYER. Prayers in a dream symbolize gratitude, success in achieving your goals, happiness, and a modest financial standing.

a. You are praying: If you appear praying alone in a place of worship, it reflects your sense of gratitude to the Creator. If you are with several others, it presages a success for your modest goals. If you appear praying alone in your house, it is a sign of continued happiness in the house. If you appear praying with other family members, it is a good sign, promising a dignified future with the minimum requirements of a modest life.

b. You see others praying: If your parents are praying, it foretells a happy marriage for you and if married, a rewarding married life. If you find your friends praying, it denotes sincerity in friendship.

PREGNANCY. Pregnancy symbolizes a difficult period surmounted by financial setbacks and illness. But it is a symbol of happy days for the aged woman. For a woman who is pregnant, this dream has no significance.

a. You are pregnant: If you are unmarried and dream of pregnancy, it forebodes difficulties arising out of your laziness. If you are just married, it suggests difficulties and unhappiness due to a bad partner. If married and with children, it foretells a financial setback and illness within the family. If you are divorced and dream of pregnancy, it means problems at home and at work. If unemployed, chances are slim for the opportunity to work. If you are aged and have such a dream, it means happy days without any form of scarcity.

b. You see others pregnant: Seeing others pregnant is a warning to plan your moves carefully and to maintain cordial relations with all.

PRISON. A prison, as its name implies, does not necessarily symbolize anything harmful. On the contrary, a prison in a subconscious state indicates freedom and happiness.

a. You see a prison: Seeing a prison suggests the imminent arrival of calmer days where you will be able to utilize your energy and talents for a constructive project. If you see people or acquaintances behind bars, it suggests positive help from friends in your hour of need. But if you see just one individual in a prison, it suggests a delay or even a disappointment in arriving at your goals.

b. You are in a prison: If with friends, it means you will be busy at least for the foreseeable future pursuing your positive tasks. If alone, again, it is a mark of disappointment.

PROFANITY. Profane language in a dream underscores a person's vulgarity. It also symbolizes terrible hardships due to one's own faults.

a. You hear profanity: If you recognize the person talking profanity, it foretells a tense situation at home with endless quarrels. If you do not recognize the person, it is a warning to lower tempers at home.

b. You use profane language: If you use such language, it foretells you will have terrible mishaps, ending in untold miseries for you and your family members. Unless you control your habits and mend your character, such a dream also foretells a downfall from which you may not recover.

PROPHET. A known prophet is the harbinger of good news and good health. A false prophet symbolizes confusion in your daily life.

a. You see a prophet: If known, popular, and loved, it is a sign assuring you of extrication from your present sorrows. If ill, there will be a gradual health recovery. It also means an appreciable change in your financial standing. A prophet's presence also foretells respect and honor for you from the society. If the prophet appears pleased or consoles you, it presages a sudden change in your life. A false prophet's appearance is considered as unfavorable, since you will not only be misguided, but you will have confusion.

b. A prophet gives you something: Receiving something from a prophet heralds the beginning of your search for a spiritual life.

PROPOSALS. Depending on who proposes and on what subject, several interpretations can be had.

a. You and the proposals: If you (a man) propose to marry a woman, while both of you are unwed, it means you will very soon find the possibilities to attain financial prosperity, and if you (a married man) propose to an unmarried woman, it speaks of your lack of a serious approach to life. If you propose to a married woman while both of you are married, it means you are still unaware of your future. If you (a woman) propose to marry a man while both of you are unwed, it means you will soon exit a monotonous life. If you (a married woman) propose to an unmarried man, it means you are not ready to accept the realities of life, and if you propose to marry a married man, it means you are not too honest in your dealings. If a blind, handicapped, or a sick woman already married proposes to marry

155

you, irrespective of whether you are married or not, and you accept the proposal, it means you will stoop as low as possible to attain your evil designs. If you refuse the proposal, it shows your abilities to control your emotions. But if a blind or a handicapped person, irrespective of the fact of whether married or not, proposes to marry you, an unwed woman, and you accept the proposal, it means you are content with your present life and if you refuse, it means your goals are unattainable. If someone proposes you a journey, it means that you will soon change your address. If someone proposes you to indulge in an unlawful act and you accept, it is a warning of an impending legal suit against you. If you refuse to accept, it means you enjoy your independence. If someone proposes you to play a game or any sport and if you accept, it denotes continued good health. If you propose to buy a property and if the response is positive, it means you will have an exceptionally good financial year.

PROSTITUTE. A prostitute symbolizes disease, quarrels, divorce, unemployment, and accidents.

a. You (a man or a woman) see a prostitute: A warning not to place too much confidence in friends. If the prostitute nears you, it is a sign of an impending disease that will require professional medical care. If she speaks with you, and if you refrain from answering her, it reflects a determination to change your character, but if you answer her, it is a sign of degradation, unemployment, and hardships.

b. You are a prostitute: An unfavorable omen foretelling a breakage in friendship, disputes with your parents, and confrontations with your spouse ultimately leading to divorce. If you dream of having relations with a person, it foretells problems at work leading to unemployment. If you are attacked or insulted, it foretells an injurious accident.

PURSE. A purse, whether empty or full, is a lucky omen. It symbolizes gains in life through one's honest efforts.

a. You see a purse: If it contains money, it foretells more to come through your labor. If it is empty, still you will gain money, but with some difficulties. If you are given a purse with money, it betokens setbacks and unhappiness. If it is an empty purse, it is a sign of encouragement.

b. You buy, lose, or find a purse: Buying a purse foresees a determination on your part to forego unlawful means in life. Losing a purse signifies your irrational approach to life while finding one means you will always find help in friends and family members for your modest projects.

PYRAMID. A pyramid symbolizes the realization of your labors. As such, it symbolizes business success and sudden riches, too.

a. You see a pyramid: If you are near the pyramid, it foretells an exceptionally happy period in which you will realize your goals. If far, it suggests a little more effort to be done. A destroyed pyramid suggests a general setback.

b. You are on a pyramid: A rare dream, presaging a success in your business. It also means you will have a fortune bequeathed to you. If you fall from a pyramid, you are being too careless.

Q

QUARRY. Any type of quarry in one's dream symbolizes hardships, loss of a lawsuit, imprisonment, and even a struggle in life. As such, it is considered an unfavorable dream.

a. You see a quarry: An empty quarry symbolizes unbearable hardships due to a loss of a lawsuit. If people are seen working in it, it foretells imprisonment due to past crimes. If you happen to recognize anybody down there, it presages misfortunes in general.

b. You are working in a quarry: Such a dream signifies your struggles in life. It also means dishonor arising from your untoward acts in society.

c. You fall in a quarry: If you fall in a quarry, it means those whom you still consider friends will be one day instrumental for your bad days. But if you manage to climb out of the quarry, it means you will be able to unaidedly return to a normal life.

QUEEN. A queen dead or alive symbolizes setbacks, financial loss, degradation, and continued hardship in one's life. A queen's presence in a dream is a bad omen.

a. You see a queen: If the queen appears to be ornately dressed, it symbolizes all forms of setbacks and a terrible financial loss from which you may not recover. If she appears with her friends or officials, it foretells ridicule and degradation due to your faulty and irresponsible behavior. If she appears feasting or at a party, it signifies continued hardships with no help in sight. A queen riding on a horse or in a carriage foretells unbearable problems at home. In short, the more pompous she appears, the deeper will be the effects of all sorts of miseries on you. A dowager empress's presence in one's dream presages separation or even a divorce. If the dowager empress speaks or even gestures at you, it is a bad omen, foretelling the death of a youth in the family. The king's presence with her neutralizes the evil effects of the dream.

b. You are a queen: An unfavorable dream denoting the gradual flowering of revenge, malice, and greed within you.

QUESTIONS. Asking questions in one's dream symbolizes the desire to find positive ways and means towards a better life and to solve your pending problems in an appropriate manner.

a. You are asking questions: If you appear to ask questions of your parents, teacher, or a friend, it symbolizes your honest desire to find the positive ways for a dignified life. Asking questions of an attorney means you are desirous of ending your unlawful ways of life. Posing questions to a priest reflects your strong religious inclinations. Asking questions of fellow workers reflects the importance you attach to spiritual values.

b. You are asked questions: Being asked questions by an attorney foretells legal problems unless you move fast enough to correct your situation; by parents, it denotes help; by friends, it denotes consolation.

QUICKSAND. Quicksand symbolizes a gradual but a continued loss in financial matters. It also symbolizes failing health, with no recovery in sight.

a. You see quicksand: If you are far away from it, it warns you to take care of your financial dealings. If near, it warns you in health matters.

b. You fall in quicksand: If you fall in quicksand but do not sink, it signifies a short setback in business and financial matters. However, if you are able to save yourself, it means you will have exceptionally good luck in business. If someone helps to pull you out, it means friends will help you out of your problems.

R

RABBI. A rabbi symbolizes truth and decency. He also symbolizes consolation, healing, good health, and a modest life.

a. You see a rabbi: If the rabbi appears conducting a religious meeting, it marks an urge within you to uphold truth and decency. If the rabbi appears casually speaking with people, you will soon receive consolation for your unhappiness. If the rabbi speaks with you, and if you are ailing, you will be at least partially healed. If in good health, you will have continued good health. If the rabbi gives you something, it is a sign of assurance of a modest and a happy life.

b. You are a rabbi: If you have ever indulged in any sort of vice or any untoward act in life and you dream of being a rabbi, it is a good sign, foretelling the beginning a new and a fruitful life somewhere in the near future.

RACE. Participation in any form of race symbolizes an uncertain life marked by confrontations and jealousies. As such, it is an unfavorable dream for those not in the profession of sports.

a. You participate in a race: If it concerns any sport event, it symbolizes an urge within you to try your luck at any goal, even if it means indulging in unlawful acts. But if you are a sports person by profession and you dream of participating in a sports event, it suggests good health. If you (not a sports person) dream of winning a race, it foretells problems and arguments with virtually one and all. If you lose the race, it symbolizes an uncertain life marked by regular confrontations and jealousies.

RAGE. Showing rage in a dream symbolizes financial loss, nervousness, undependable friends, and betrayal in love. As such, it is an unfavorable dream.

a. You show rage: If you appear to show rage at your place of business, it foretells a loss due to your improper attention towards your profession. If it is at work, it presages quarrels there leading to unemployment. If it is towards your friends, it means a breakage in friendship. If your rage is directed against your lover, it spells separation, and if you show rage to your spouse, it betokens a divorce.

b. Others show you rage: If your lover rages at you, it means you will eventually be a betrayer; if it is your parents, you are being too irresponsible; and if it is your brother or sister, it foretells a long period of unhappiness marked by unemployment.

RAIN. Light showers symbolize a new beginning for the better. Torrential rains symbolize setbacks due to faulty planning and bad associates.

a. You see rain: Light showers are a token of good omen. They symbolize an end to your minor worries and foretell the beginning of a new life within the next few days. They also suggest your sudden meeting with a person who will greatly influence your life towards better days. Torrential rains foretell brief financial setbacks resulting from faulty planning. If floods appear to be forming, it signifies bad associates who will try to ruin you.

b. You stand under rain: If you appear soaked, it means you will have to labor hard to realize even a small project, but if the rain does not seem to make you wet or if you have an umbrella, you will, however with a delay, realize your goals.

RECEIVING. Receiving a gift, praise, punishment, news, or an order has various significances depending on the characteristics of things received.

a. You receive something: If it is a gift, your labors will soon be appreciated either through a promotion or recognition from a supporter. If you appear to have received punishment from a court, it means you have to be careful in your dealings with acquaintances or those concerned with you. If it is a punishment at work, such as a demotion or layoff, it presages a quarrel with your employer. If you receive pleasant news, beware of false promises. If the news is unpleasant, it means you will have to face your difficult situation alone. If it is an order, whether pleasant or otherwise, it is a good sign, signalling a sudden change in your life, essentially benefitting you. Any praise received is a sign of encouragement.

RECOVERING (a thing, or from illness). Recovering anything, whether an object, from illness, or from a financial setback, is considered a favorable omen.

a. You recover an object: If you recover an object you lost or forgot long ago and if it has any value for you, it foretells an imminent recovery from a previous loss. If you appear to recover medication from any place, it is a good sign, meaning you will recover from an illness, if any.

b. You recover from illness: If you are ill and you dream of recovery, it is a contrary dream suggesting continued ill health due to your irresponsibility vis-à-vis your ailment.

REMARRYING. Remarrying signifies both favorable as well as unfavorable developments. This is a dream for those already divorced, a widow or widower.

a. You are remarrying: If you are already married and dream of being just married, it denotes a delicate situation with your spouse in the next few days. If you are divorced and dream of remarrying an old person who is a widow or widower, it means continued difficulties and financial losses to the brink of bankruptcy. If your spouse has not been married like you before, it heralds a good beginning in life. If you (a widow) dream of remarrying a widower or vice versa, it is a good sign of a long and healthy life.

b. You remarry your own ex-spouse: A rare dream underscoring your period of isolation and unhappiness. If you dream of remarrying your ex-spouse, it foretells a long period of mental stress and underscores your extremely unhappy state.

RESTAURANT. Depending on what happens in a restaurant and your situation in it, an interpretation can be had.

a. You see a restaurant: Just seeing a restaurant from near or at a distance symbolizes your lonely and unhappy life. If you enter the restaurant and see a crowd, it suggests a busy schedule, which will be beneficial to you. If the restaurant appears empty, it denotes false promises by undependable friends.

b. You own a restaurant: Whether you fully or partially own a restaurant in a dream, it suggests that good days are not far away where you will at least have the average comforts of life.

RESULT. Awaiting any result in a dream symbolizes anxiety, mental stress, and even a temporary financial setback.

a. You are awaiting a result: If it is the result of a test or examination, it underscores your anxiety for the moment. If in real life you are seeking a divorce and you are awaiting its outcome, it suggests mental stress currently afflicting you. If you are an expecting mother and dream the results of birth, it shows your impatience in life. If you are expecting the results of a lawsuit, it denotes a temporary financial setback.

b. You receive a result: If you (a woman) dream of a negative answer to any result you are expecting, you will have a satisfying one. On the contrary, for a man, a negative result or a positive result bears the same significance.

REUNION (REUNITING with friends, family members). A reunion of friends, relatives, business partners, and school mates symbolizes happiness, renewed vigor in general, success in business, an end to misunderstanding and even animosity between friends and family members. Any anger or quarrel during a reunion has negative results.

a. You witness a reunion: Witnessing any reunion symbolizes joy and happiness within you and all your family members.

b. You participate in a reunion: If it is a reunion with friends whom you have not seen for a long time, it means encouragement and renewed vigor for you to begin a new phase in life. If during the reunion you are offered a gift, if is a sure sign of success either in business or at the place of work. If it is a reunion with former school mates, it is a good sign of continued good health and an expansion of your professional activities. If you have a reunion with your ex-business partners, it foretells moral and financial help to start a business, or if you are continuing in business, a sudden profit. If you have a reunion with your family members, it suggests an imminent end to misunderstandings.

RIDING (any animal). A very favorable dream. Riding symbolizes profit in business, dependable friends, success in love and marriage, and sound health.

a. You are riding: If you are riding a horse, it denotes fortunes through a business career. Riding a mule or a donkey presages a meeting with persons who will be of extensive use. Riding with your spouse on any animal signifies a happy married life, while with your lover, it suggests a stable and a fruitful marriage. Riding an ordinary camel foretells a short travel that if not gainful will not be too useless, while riding a "double-humped camel" (a rare dream) promises sudden gains both through business as well as inheritance.

b. You see others riding: Seeing anyone, whether related to you or not, is a good and a lucky sign, for it foretells help and assistance with all your problems.

RING. A ring symbolizes both a favorable as well as an unfavorable development. Depending on the situation of the ring and you, an interpretation can be had.

a. You and a ring: If you give a ring to a person whom you adore in heart and which is a one-sided love affair, that person, apart from never marrying you, will have a terrible marriage. But if you dream of giving a ring to your partner with whom you share common love, it means an early and a good marriage. Losing, having lost, or breaking your marriage ring foretells a delicate situation with your spouse due to baseless arguments. However, finding (if you have lost your ring in real life) your ring foretells a happy married life.

RIVER. A river symbolizes true love and happiness. At the same time, depending on the situation of the river, it symbolizes quarrels and misunderstandings.

a. You see a river: A clean and a lucidly flowing river symbolizes true love with your partner or spouse. If you take a dip in the river, it is a good sign, indicating continued joy and happiness within you. A clean river, with an uneven flow or with rocks, symbolizes several small obstacles in your path that could be overcome with a little wisdom. A dirty or a swift-flowing river foretells a temporary setback due to small errors committed in the past. If you appear to take a dip or just touch the water, it means you are wasting time on unrealistic projects. Be more realistic!

b. A river is suddenly formed near your house: A good dream promising a sudden change in your life, which will greatly benefit you.

ROAD. A road, depending on its construction and shape, symbolizes favorable as well as unfavorable developments.

a. You see a road: If it is a straight and a wide road, it signifies an easy path towards realizing your aims in life. A narrow and a winding road spells a pleasant surprise within the next few days, while a narrow gravel road signifies the hardships you are presently undergoing. A stone-cobbled road, whether narrow or wide, whether straight or winding, promises fruitful results to your honest labors in life.

ROBBERY. Any form of robbery, whether of an expensive material or even eatables, symbolizes a nervous behavior, lack of self-control, indulgence in vice, and a lawsuit.

a. You see a robbery: Seeing a robbery symbolizes nervous and angry behavior. Being robbed in a dream underscores your lack of self-control, which may lead you to problems unless you move ahead to check yourself.

b. You participate in a robbery or rob alone: Participating in a robbery with others reflects your plans to indulge in vice while robbing alone foretells a lawsuit against you. If you are already facing a lawsuit, the case will end against you.

ROCKS. Rocks, whether medium or large, symbolize obstacles and also problems, chiefly due to conspiracies and jealousies by one's own acquaintances mistakenly considered as friends.

a. You see rocks: If the rocks appear in front of your path while riding, walking, or driving, it symbolizes obstacles, problems, and even setbacks, created due to conspiracies. However, if you manage to continue your way by moving between them, onward in your journey, your problems will be short-lived. But if you are not able to traverse between them, it suggests obstacles that have to be overcome through wisdom.

b. You climb a huge rock: Climbing a huge rock suggests your potential to begin a new life with a little help. Falling from a rock foretells a failure if you have extravagant projects.

ROOF (any form of roof offering temporary shelter). Any roof in a dream symbolizes protection and sanctuary from harm. It also symbolizes a sudden help from unexpected quarters, greatly relieving one from present plights.

a. You see a roof: Just seeing a roof foretells an occasion where you will find good and helpful friends. If you appear to stand under a roof, it suggests protection of your interests by dependable and honest friends or family members. If you see a collapsed roof, it foretells a failure due to incorrect planning.

b. You are building a roof: Constructing a roof denotes a favorable business venture. If not in business, it suggests an appreciable employment proposal with much better conditions. If you appear to have just completed a roof, it denotes good rewards for your honest labors.

ROPE. A rope symbolizes temporary confinement to one's place, setbacks, and inability to perform any work due to stress.

a. You see a rope: Just seeing a rope lying down or hanging or even in a coil serves as a warning to be on the guard so as not to be confronted by setbacks due to minor errors.

b. You appear tied by a rope: Such a dream foretells major obstacles due to bad planning. It also suggests a complete halt to your business activity and denotes your inability to function due to mental stress arising out of your past mistakes. Hasten to seek wise and professional counsel. If you manage to free yourself, you will regain your abilities once more.

c. You tie someone with a rope: Such a dream underscores your angry mood and fickle behavior. Meditate and pray.

RUNNING. Depending on the reasons for your running, an interpretation can be had.

a. You are running: If you are running away from danger, it denotes your sagacious character. If you are running to find or get something, it denotes your constructive behavior. If you are running or hastening to indulge in any untoward act, it suggests uncertainty and even failure. If you appear running for exercise, it denotes a healthy life coupled with continued good health. If you fall while running, it means you are not as careful as you should be.

b. You see others running: Seeing others running normally is an encouraging sign for you to continue your attempts until you arrive at your aim in life. Seeing a thief or a criminal running is a warning to beware of undesired acquaintances.

S

SABRE. A sabre symbolizes anger, revenge, and inconsistencies in one's dealings.

a. You see a sabre: If sheathed, it is a timely warning to control your temper and to do away with the vindictive nature within you. If unsheathed or you appear to be holding one, it foretells violence through heated arguments.

b. You attack someone with a sabre: Attacking someone with a sabre foretells a lawsuit in the future much to your disadvantage. Unless you seek professional help to calm down your feelings and temper, you will be faced with an indefinite period of hardships.

c. You are presented with a sabre: Being presented with a sabre denotes you are being guided and motivated by untrustworthy elements whom you unfortunately consider friends. If you happen to recognize the person presenting you the sabre, it would be to your benefit to disassociate yourself from that person.

d. You are attacked with a sabre: Being attacked with a sabre means that you have to be on your guard.

SACK. A sack symbolizes surprises both favorable as well as otherwise. Depending on the situation and objects within the sack, an interpretation can be had.

a. You see a sack: If the sack is small and tied up, it denotes a pleasant surprise, perhaps a positive reply to your requests. If the sack is open and filled with useful objects, it means a small gift or modest help is on the way. If the sack is big and closed, it denotes a fruitful proposal that may positively affect your life. If it is open and empty, it means you have to labor much to arrive at your ambitions. If it contains useful or even useless objects in it, it means you will be facilitated towards your aims, thanks to the presence of dependable friends.

b. You are presented a sack with valuables: This is a dream warning you to refrain from depending too much on other people's help, since it will serve to dissuade you from being independent. Such a dream also betokens a state of poverty in later periods in life.

SADDLE. A saddle symbolizes hard work, patience, and a dislike for a pompous life.

a. You see a saddle: If mounted on a horse, it suggests a short and a fruitful journey. If it is placed on a stand, it denotes a lot has to be accomplished before you witness a slight change in your life. If the saddle is lying on the ground, it underscores your patience in life.

b. You are repairing or making a saddle: Repairing a saddle means you are quite contented with what you have while making a saddle underlines your dislike for a pompous life. It also underscores your honest ways in life.

SAFE (for money or valuables). A safe symbolizes isolation and unhappiness.

a. You see a safe: A closed safe denotes your miserly character devoid of any compassion. An open safe with valuables within it symbolizes your indifference to life while an empty one denotes your willingness to go to any extremes to gain riches.

b. You see a robbed safe: A safe appearing to have been broken through by robbers suggests an unhappy period conspicuously marked by isolation.

SAILING. Sailing symbolizes success and prosperity in general. It also symbolizes a happy family with a devoted spouse.

a. You are sailing: If you appear to be sailing in the sea in a small boat, it denotes success in business. If the boat appears quite large with opened sails, it symbolizes prosperity in general in your day-to-day affairs. If you appear to be managing your boat alone, it means you will unaidedly realize your ambitions. If your family members also appear to be with you, apart from realizing your ambitions, you will have a happy married life together with a devoted spouse.

b. You see others sailing: A good sign encouraging you to continue your efforts, for success will be ultimately yours.

SAINT. A saint's presence in one's dream, whether in the form of a picture or as visualized through beliefs and traditions, is an exceptionally wonderful sign. His or her presence symbolizes truth and justice, healing, an end to sufferings and miseries, and a modest life marked with spiritual values. It is commonly accepted that those dreaming of saints must not relate their dream to others.

a. You see a saint: If the saint appears to bless you or give you affection or grace, it means several things at one time. If you have a lawsuit against you and feel wronged, justice will be meted in your favor. If you are ill or with a failing health, you will recover, much to the surprise of those around you. If you are unhappy or experiencing hardships, you will have better days.

b. A saint gives you something or talks with you: A saint giving you something means you will have a modest life with spiritual values while a saint talking to you denotes encouragement and safety from harm.

SALT. Salt symbolizes help, consolation, and virtue.

a. You see salt: Whether in a packet, a jar, or in a plate, salt foretells the imminent arrival of help to save you from further distress. If you are offered salt by a person whom you recognize, that very person will help you in your hour of need. If you do not recognize him, you will shortly befriend a person who will be of immense use. If you offer salt to someone, it denotes the strong degree of virtue within you.

b. You buy or sell salt: Buying salt indicates guests whom you will greatly appreciate while selling salt means you will shortly help a family experiencing hardships.

SAND. Sand symbolizes obstacles and difficulties in one's life. As such, it is considered an unfavorable dream.

a. You see sand: If you have any projects in mind, make sure to plan them properly. If you are planning to buy or sell something, postpone it for at least a fortnight. If planning to make a business trip, consider the advantages and disadvantages well in advance.

b. You find yourself on a sandy area: Such a dream foretells further difficulties you will face as a result of previous mishaps in business and social life.

SAVING (a life). Saving someone's life or being saved is a favorable omen. It symbolizes a life free from harm or dangers. It also symbolizes being saved from poverty, illness, and even a lawsuit.

a. You are being saved: If you dream of drowning and appear being saved, it means impersonal forces or sheer luck will steer you away from present dangers haunting you. If you are falling down from a slope or any height and you appear saved, it means your own family members will bail you out from your present financial difficulties. If you dream of any vehicle trying to run you over and if you suddenly appear saved, it suggests your own skills and potentials will finally help you overcome your present bad days. If you are ailing and you dream of being saved from a person attempting to kill you, it suggests a recovery. If your father appears to save you from any danger, it foretells a safe life. If you are faced with a lawsuit and your father saves you from an imminent danger to your life, justice would end in your favor.

b. You save somebody: Saving any person in your dream symbolizes your capacity to achieve your ambitions whether sooner or later. But if you appear to save your parents or any aged person, it is a wonderful sign, promising a long healthy life with enough riches to spare to those unfortunate. Saving an animal either from drowning or being killed is a wonderful omen, suggesting a life free from any harm.

SCHOOL. Any school, whether primary, secondary, or advanced, symbolizes chances and opportunities for one to start an altogether new life. It also symbolizes help and guidance both from family members as well as friends.

a. You see a school: If there are students in the school, it is a good sign, encouraging you to plan alternatives in life. If the students appear in the school yard, it is a sign of relief from your present worries. If you happen to see a kindergarten school with little children, it means you have all the possibilities within you to virtually attain your goals in a short time. An empty school signifies futile attempts at unrealistic projects.

b. You are in a school: If you suddenly find yourself back at school and studying again in one of the classes you favored the most, it is an exceptionally good sign of bright prospects in life marked by enough wealth. Being talked to by one of your favorite teachers denotes help and assistance in getting a start in life.

SCISSORS. Scissors in a dream symbolize both a favorable and an unfavorable development, mostly within the family.

a. You see scissors: If you (a married woman) see scissors, it foretells a heated argument with your husband, ending in sour relations for at least a hundred days while for an unmarried one, it presages an early and a happy marriage. If you happen to threaten anyone with scissors, it is a sign of nervousness within you. If you (a married or an unmarried man) dream of scissors, it foretells quarrels with those around you.

b. You use scissors: Using scissors for a constructive purpose denotes you will soon execute your plans, which could be very beneficial to you. But if you appear to destroy any article with scissors, it underlines your destructive character.

SELLING (an object or property). Selling an object or property in one's dream, if due to poverty or need for money and for business reasons, has various significances, favorable as well as otherwise.

a. You are selling: Selling a house or property for business reasons foretells an appreciable profit in business, or if employed, it denotes a promotion. If you appear to sell for reasons of need for money, it denotes a short financial setback. Selling any animal in your dream denotes your desire to make profits through any channel, whether legal or otherwise. Selling any object means you are undergoing a difficult period.

b. You sell other people's property: Selling other people's property or objects underscores your fraudulent ways in life. It also means it will be virtually difficult for you to mend your ways. Meditation and regular visits to a place of worship will greatly help you overcome such a trend in life.

SHARPENING. Sharpening any object of utility, such as a knife, scissors, or a razor with a constructive purpose, symbolizes honest efforts and modest gains in life.

a. You are sharpening an object: Such a dream foretells commencement of an ambitious dream with honest efforts within the next thirty days, which will essentially change your life for the better.

b. You are sharpening an offensive object: Sharpening such objects like a knife or a razor for criminal intentions foretells great losses in your life, particularly business or professional, which will drastically affect your character. Take great pains to mend your ways in life.

SHEPHERD. A shepherd symbolizes success in business and profession. A shepherd also symbolizes happiness and cordial relations with all.

a. You see a shepherd: A shepherd standing idly or lying down signifies irresponsibility while if he appears tending his flock, it suggests hectic activities in the next few days for which you will have every reason to celebrate.

b. You are a shepherd: Becoming a shepherd in your dream means you are contented with life while being with a flock speaks of your strong desire to be friendly with all. It also symbolizes happiness at home.

SHIELD. A shield is a symbol of recovery from health and financial loss, protection from harm, and a good married life.

a. You see a shield: A shield, lying anywhere, symbolizes hope and is also a sign of moral encouragement.

b. You and a shield: If you appear to hold a shield, it means you are finally determined to try your hand at a project. If you are experiencing financial hardships, you will have better days. If you are faced with problems at home, the situation will ameliorate. And if your life appears to be in any sort of danger, you will have safety.

SHIP. A ship, depending on its type and position, has both favorable as well as unfavorable significances.

a. You see a ship: A passenger ship sailing smoothly signifies a perfect concord within the family while a ship in a stormy sea denotes impending disputes and arguments leading to unhappiness. A cargo ship sailing calmly denotes prospects in business and happiness at work while one battling heavy waves denotes uncertainty, loss due to illogical temptations, and bad guidance from those masquerading as friends and supporters. A naval ship, whether in calm or stormy waters, also denotes uncertainty but due to your own lack of understanding.

b. You are on a ship: Being on any ship with smooth sailing denotes you have been playing your modest part quite well in life and things will go well for the foreseeable future. If the ship appears tilting due to choppy waters, it means extra care is warranted.

SHIPWRECK. A shipwreck symbolizes disasters due to improper management and irresponsibility. It also symbolizes great financial losses and even bankruptcy.

a. You see a shipwreck: A half-submerged ship warns of an impending loss and finally the closure of your business or profession due to improper management and irresponsibility. A sunk ship visible below the waters is a strong warning to immediately adopt a new strategy where profession is concerned. A shipwreck on a coast symbolizes a great financial loss leading to bankruptcy.

b. You are in a shipwreck: If you find yourself in a wrecked ship under the water, which is quite strange and rare, it denotes no further possibility to continue in business, but if you are on a shipwreck on the coast, extensive efforts will ultimately make you successful.

SHIRT. A shirt symbolizes personality and general situation in one's life.

a. You see a shirt: A torn shirt denotes defamation and conspiracies through jealousies. A clean shirt with any single bright color foretells a much better life through your own efforts. A multicolored shirt reflects your perplexed and fickle nature.

b. You have a shirt on you: If you appear wearing any dark-colored clothes, you appear to have difficulty in understanding or planning the bare necessities in life. If you are wearing a black shirt, you are not as frank as you claim. However, wearing a bright-colored shirt indicates gifts and even help from friends.

c. You buy a shirt: Buying a bright-colored shirt denotes your desire to once more enter into a dignified way in life. But buying a black-colored shirt foretells regrets at your own shortcomings.

SHOES. Shoes, depending on their description and their situation vis-à-vis you, signify both favorable as well as unfavorable developments in one's life.

a. You and shoes: If you see new shoes all around you, it is a sign of a long and a useless journey while old and worn shoes symbolize meeting with friends whom you have not seen for ages. Putting on your shoes means you will make new efforts to compensate a previous failure while removing your shoes signifies a hard-earned rest.

b. You buy or sell shoes: Buying shoes means you are planning a short journey that will bring you modest gains while appearing to sell shoes means you will have a contented life.

SHOP. The significance of a shop solely depends on the type of business it conducts. Accordingly, favorable as well as unfavorable signs could be inferred.

a. You see a shop: A butcher's shop foretells an angry confrontation with your friends and even family members. A cloth shop presages a meeting with a person who will be of immense help. A shop selling fruits and vegetables denotes useful and dependable guests. A money lender's shop signifies several creditors. A coffee shop signifies a hard-earned rest while a shop selling cakes and sweets foretells a happy reunion with friends or family members. A wine shop denotes a good cause for celebration while a printing shop or a shop selling books denotes success in your career either as a writer, a consultant, or a teacher. Seeing a restaurant symbolizes the unhappy situation within you (see Restaurant).

b. You enter a shop: Entering any shop except that of a money lender is a good omen, denoting average prosperity. Entering a money lender's shop signifies a financial loss due to your own carelessness.

c. You own a shop: Owning a shop presages good days are nearing, particularly if it is a restaurant.

d. You work in a shop: Working in a shop signifies a certain degree of prosperity until you achieve an average standard of life.

SHORE. Shores of a sea or lake or a river bank symbolize idleness, uncertainty, and hopelessness.

a. You see a shoreline: A shore near or far means you have to create a determination within you to begin a constructive future. In fact, just seeing any shore underscores the deep degree of hopelessness embedded within you.

b. You are on the shores: If standing or sitting idly, it means you have not yet discovered the positive potential within you, but if you appear to walk as if in search for something, it is a favorable sign promising some constructive steps by you. Sleeping on a shore denotes your feeling of uncertainty. Stand up and face the challenges in life with courage, patience, and honesty.

SILK. Silk is a symbol of success in your ambitions. It is also a symbol of a wealthy partner in life.

a. You see silk: Whether cloth, clothes, or in any form, it symbolizes a gradual success to your ambitions.

b. You buy silk: Buying silk material foretells sudden financial gains while presenting to someone or receiving them as a gift presages marriage to a wealthy spouse. If already married, your spouse will become quite rich.

SILVER. Silver in any form symbolizes promotion in work, good business, and a good marriage. It also symbolizes harmony in the family.

a. You see silver: Whether a silver coin, ingot, or silverware, it suggests an imminent promotion at work. If in business, it means success. If you touch any silver item, it is a good sign, promising an average life together with a stable and a good marriage.

b. You buy silver: Buying a silver coin denotes a forthcoming marriage of relatives while buying ingots means a perfect harmony with your spouse and parents. Buying silverware by those married heralds the marriage of a brother or a sister. If you are unmarried, it suggests your own marriage to a wealthy person.

SINGING. Singing in a dream predicts a bitter period marked with unhappiness at home and work, unemployment, and a financial setback.

a. You are singing: If you appear to be singing softly, it predicts a bitter period marked with disputes and disagreements with your spouse. If unmarried, you will quarrel with your lover. If alone, you will receive disappointing news from your parents. If you appear to be singing loudly, it foretells bitter news, perhaps about dismissal from work. Such a dream also predicts a financial setback.

b. You hear others singing: Hearing any person singing betokens a temporary failure, but with the required skill and patience, you could avert it.

SINKING. Sinking symbolizes loss, bankruptcy, and failure.

a. You see a vessel sinking: If it is a cargo ship in the act of sinking, it suggests a terrible financial loss and perhaps bankruptcy due to your own faults. A sinking passenger ship denotes a breakage in partnership and even friends. A naval vessel sinking suggests the hopelessness within you. A small dinghy or a boat sinking foretells a temporary failure due to bad acquaintances. A fully submerged (just below the water line but not on the bottom of the ocean floor) vessel foretells a new beginning in life whose benefits will solely depend on your correct approach to life and careful planning.

b. You appear sinking with a boat: Such a dream warns of impending problems if you do not move fast enough to evaluate your present plans. It also warns of undesirable characters pretending to be friends. If through some miracle the boat is saved and the ship gains its balance, your own efforts will extricate you from your problems. Be more realistic.

SKELETON. A skeleton symbolizes disease, death, and poverty. As such, it is considered an extremely bad omen.

a. You see a skeleton: A skeleton strewn in pieces around betokens an incurable disease followed by death. If the bones appear to be properly connected to each other, it denotes financial loss and poverty in later periods of life. If the skeleton makes some gestures or even nears you, it forebodes dangers you are unaware of. But if you appear frightened and jump in your sleep, there is no significance to the dream.

b. You become a skeleton: A rare dream signifying misfortunes of all kinds ultimately driving you insane.

SKULL. A skull symbolizes ill health, an unhappy period, and a loss of life in the family.

a. You see a skull. A fallen skull is a harbinger of ill health. To those not enjoying good health, it indicates a worsening condition unless medical help is timely sought. If you touch or lift the skull, it foretells an unhappy period marked with constant quarrels. Finding a skull while digging means you will have pleasant news.

b. Somebody has a skull: If you see a person holding a skull in his hands, it foretells violence around you, though not necessarily affecting you, where death may be caused.

SKY. Depending on the situation of the sky, several favorable significances could be noted.

a. You see the sky: A clear and a blue sky foretells a progressive movement towards a prosperous life. If you appear seeing it endlessly, it underscores your fiercely incorruptible ways in life. Such a dream also foretells honors from the society for your hard and honest labors. It also means success in virtually every project you try your hand at. If the sky appears cloudy or gray, it denotes a temporary frustration to your efforts caused by haste and nervousness. It also foretells petty misunderstandings within the family.

b. You appear as if you are floating in the sky: A rare and a wonderful dream, signifying an end to all afflictions and unhappiness.

SMOKE. Smoke symbolizes family disputes, separation, and breakage in friendship.

a. You see smoke: If you see gray smoke, it symbolizes an impending dispute with your parents. Gradually rising black smoke means great care has to be taken to prevent quarrels with your spouse. A fast-rising and spreading black smoke spells violence with your spouse ending in separation.

b. You are in the midst of smoke: Being caught in smoke means you will have an unpleasant argument with a friend, which will break up the friendship.

SNOW. Snow symbolizes a forthcoming marriage, financial gains, promotion at work, opportunities, and dependable friends. As such, it is considered a favorable dream.

a. You see snow: If you see snow falling, you will very soon find the right person in your life. If you see snow on the ground, it denotes all possibilities for an extremely pleasant surprise, perhaps a financial gain either through business or a free amount from a family member. Hardened snow reflects a delay in realizing your ambitions. Walking on the snow foretells wonderful proposals for employment, or if already employed, it presages a promotion with honors. Running on the snow assures you of help from your parents. Unclear slush signifies an end to an unhappy period.

b. You see someone fallen on the snow: This is a warning to use your imagination properly and be more realistic.

c. You fall on the snow: If you appear to fall on the snow, it is a warning to properly select your friends.

SOAP. Soap symbolizes a new beginning, an end to a bitter period, and recovery of health.

a You see soap: Just seeing a cake of soap around signifies you are about to start a new activity in life. If you touch it, the project could crystallize into a beneficial future for you. If you use the soap on your hands or face, it means the washing away of your bitter past. It also means an appreciable recovery in health.

b. You buy soap: Buying soap reflects your strong intentions to change your life. It also means an intention to seek a good business partner.

SOLDIERS. A soldier symbolizes encouragement, a modest life, good health, and honesty.

a. You see soldiers: One or more soldiers in your dream serves as a moral encouragement. A soldier on guard duty suggests a peaceful and a modest life. Soldiers parading means you may soon have good reasons to celebrate a modest gain. Arguing with a soldier presages disputes with your own family members, probably with your father or brother. Quarreling with a soldier betokens a lawsuit. Seeing a dead soldier means uncertainty. Soldiers at war foretells a good surprise.

b. You are a soldier: If you dream you are a soldier, it underscores your good health and honesty. Being in the act of putting on a uniform or being inducted as a soldier reflects your dislike for vice.

SON. A son symbolizes help and support. He also symbolizes prosperity and the realization of ambitions.

a. You see your son: If you do have a son and see him, it is an assurance of help. If you see your eldest son, it means you will have peace and calm in your later days. If you do not have a son but dream of having one, it symbolizes unexpected gains and prosperity. If he gives you something, it suggests the realization of your ambitions through help from unexpected quarters.

b. You quarrel with your son: Whether you have a son or not, if you appear to quarrel with him, it means you are being too rash with your own friends and supporters.

SPEAR. A spear symbolizes an easily agitated and nervous nature. It also symbolizes dissatisfaction at home, at work, and with friends.

a. You see a spear: An abnormally long spear denotes your easily agitated and nervous nature. If you have any plans for a project or a trip, postpone it for at least a fortnight. A normal spear reflects your deep animosity towards someone you dislike for a long period.

b. You have a spear: Having a spear in your hand signals an impending quarrel that could end in a lawsuit. Threatening someone or even injuring someone with a spear presages loss in a legal procedure ending in a short-term imprisonment.

c. You are given a spear: Such a dream indicates evil temptations to arrive at a certain goal through unfair and even criminal means. Control your sinful desires through prayers.

STABLE. A stable symbolizes a breakthrough in business, a continued happy life, and dependable friends.

a. You see a stable: A stable with any single animal foretells a breakthrough in your business, while if full of cows, sheep, or horses, it foretells a modest fortune with a continued happy life. A stable full of donkeys indicates tiresome efforts even to have a modest gain. A stable full of various animals promises new and dependable friends.

b. You build a stable: Building or even repairing a stable denotes your great will to continue a traditional life.

STAIRS. A staircase symbolizes surprises, both favorable as well as otherwise. Depending on the situation of the stairs and you and the surroundings, an interpretation can be had.

a. You see stairs: A narrow winding stair symbolizes a favorable surprise while a narrow and a straight stair betokens the opposite. If you see a door at the end of any stairs, it means the future is appreciably bright. If on reaching the end of a staircase you open a door and enter an empty room, it means your efforts are not being directed properly, but if you meet friendly people inside, it is a sure sign of prosperity and happiness.

b. You fall from the stairs: Falling from a staircase betokens a general loss, while being deliberately pushed down by others signifies conspiracies by acquaintances that will, however, be futile. Choose your friends with great care.

STARS. Stars symbolize success in business, advancement in work, good health, and a good marriage.

a. You see stars: Bright and shining stars spell happy moments, with a sudden profit in business as well as expansion in your profession. Dull stars suggest much has to be done to achieve even a simple project. If the stars appear "very near," it denotes continued good health together with a good marriage in the near future. If already married, it reflects a perfect concord.

b. You see falling stars: Falling stars denote a sudden failure coupled with failing health. They also indicate misunderstandings with your spouse and even children, if any.

STARVATION. A contrary dream symbolizing plenty, prosperity, and property. It also symbolizes enough riches to donate to the needy.

a. You are starving: If you appear starving and in utter poverty, such a dream heralds an excellent beginning with plenty of riches together with property and continued prosperity. If you dream to be starving to such an extent that death appears near, it foretells a life where you will be able to realize your childhood ambitions to help one and all in need. If someone appears to pity you, it underscores your selfless service to mankind.

b. You see others starving: If you see your parents starving, they shall have a contented life; if they are your brothers or sisters, they will prosper beside you. Seeing friends starving denotes honest and reliable friends. Helping those starving once again underscores your human nature.

STATUE. A statue, depending on its posture, has several messages. The situation of the statue and its material play an important part in determining a favorable as well as an unfavorable significance.

a. You see a statue: If you see a statue that you have been often looking at in your conscious state, it means that you are quite consistent in following your goals. If you do not appear to identify the statue, the posture of the statue must be considered. A calm, well-appearing, or friendly-faced statue denotes a certain degree of success due to the timely help of dependable friends while an angry-appearing one, chipped, broken, or virtually destroyed warns of problems in general. A marble statue signifies business success, a stone one denotes good health, while a bronze one means misunderstandings with your spouse. A golden statue signifies recklessness while one made of clay or plaster betokens illness, although not dangerous.

STITCHING. Stitching symbolizes a constructive approach towards solving one's problems. As such, it symbolizes the possibilities to inch ahead gradually towards normalcy after a long period of continued setbacks and failures.

a. You are stitching: If you appear stitching any torn clothes, it reflects your desire to rise in dignity through hard labor. If you appear stitching any form of a bag, it is a hopeful sign, foretelling you are inching forward slowly and steadily towards your goal.

b. You see others stitching: Seeing others stitching is an encouraging sign, prompting you to make efforts towards your goals rather than to be hopeless.

STOCKINGS. Depending on whether a man or a woman sees stockings in a dream, they symbolize disappointments and success in love matters, extravagance, and even poverty.

a. You (a woman) see stockings: If the stockings are new or good, it symbolizes your conquest in love matters. If you appear to be putting them on, it means you will have a unique husband. If you see torn or laddered stockings, it means you will find disappointment in love at a later period.

b. You (a man) see stockings: Whether the stockings are old and torn or good, it underscores your extravagances and irresponsibilities in life. Mending torn stockings betokens a difficult financial situation ultimately leading to bankruptcy.

c. You buy stockings: Buying stockings underscores your awareness for future needs. It also underscores great care and even readiness to meet any challenge in life.

STRAW. Straw, depending on its situation, symbolizes profits, loss, sorrow, and disappointment.

a. You see straw: Straw lying uncut symbolizes profits in business or a better living standard only if you are quite reticent and flexible. Cut straw on the field betokens loss through sheer negligence. Straw in bales heaped together signifies disappointment in your love affair. If you are married, it signifies disputes with your spouse. Straw bales lying apart in the field foretell a separation leading to divorce.

b. You see straw burning: Such a dream foretells sorrow and anguish following the results of your untoward acts in life. It also presages dishonor and disgrace. If you manage to fight the fire alone, it symbolizes a last-minute urge to change into a new leaf. If others appear to help you fight the blaze, you will receive wise counsel and even assistance to begin a new life. If the fire appears to be put out without much damage to the straw, it foretells a timely and a sagacious move with a little luck will save you the perils of disgrace.

SUICIDE. Suicide in a dream symbolizes lost hope, revenge, and nervousness. It is also a sign of an exceedingly bad marriage.

a. You commit suicide: Such a dream underscores your feelings as having totally lost all hopes after a series of failures. If you think about committing suicide, it means you nurture deep animosity against a person whom you profoundly detest. Practice forgiveness and tolerance through prayers and meditation.

b. You see others committing suicide: Such a dream reflects your nervousness and the unfavorable results of a hasty decision.

SWIMMING. Swimming symbolizes success in your modest

projects. It is also a sign of good health and friendly relations. Depending on your situation, swimming also denotes setbacks.

a. You are swimming: If you are swimming in a small pond or a pool, it denotes a success in your modest projects. In a calm river, it denotes a good health while in a turbulent river, it foretells several minor disputes that will bring depression and health problems. Swimming in a sea or ocean foretells beneficial trips to coastal regions that will be advantageous.

b. You find difficulty while swimming: If you find difficulty while swimming or appear in danger of drowning, it means you will have to experience a series of difficulties or setbacks before being able to succeed in your undertakings. If someone appears to help you, it means assistance to facilitate your efforts towards your goals. If you feel you have drowned and violently shake in your sleep, there is no further significance to the dream, since it could be considered as organic.

SWORD. A sword symbolizes inconsistency in one's attitude, nervousness, and even a violent temper. It also symbolizes loss and unemployment.

a. You see a sword: A large sword symbolizes your undependable behavior. It also signifies the violence within you. If you pick up or hold a sword, it signifies an impending quarrel ending in violence. If you threaten someone with a sword, it foretells a judicial procedure against you. If you harm someone with a sword, it foretells a loss in a lawsuit ending in a prison term. Being struck by a sword means quarrels at home and at work often ending in unemployment.

b. You buy or sell a sword: Buying a sword signifies your intentional desire to enter the world of crime, while selling it denotes your desire to end a life full of vice and enter into a meaningful life.

T

TABLE. A table, depending on its situation, symbolizes developments mostly favorable.

a. You and a table: A large table with several chairs unoccupied suggests an imminent meeting with friends or family members that will greatly affect your situation for the better. If you have bickerings with your spouse and have such a dream, it foretells a satisfactory end to your domestic problems. An empty table without chairs means much has to be done to achieve a little gain. A table spread out as if for dinner suggests a happy domestic situation. A table stet up for tea with pastries denotes good and dependable friends. A table for two suggests an extremely good marriage (if married) and for the unmarried, it means a good partner. A table with broken crockeries and broken bottles suggests misunderstandings between friends, and if married, it means quarrels within the family but not necessarily with your spouse. A table with empty plates or unworthy items on it reflects the deep perplexity within you. A table full of flowers lying on it spells mourning while if in a vase or a holder, it foretells success in your undertakings.

TAILOR. A tailor symbolizes ability, craftsmanship, and a life free of vice.

a. You see a tailor: If the tailor appears to be working, it is a good sign, encouraging you to use your talents in a constructive manner. If the tailor appears sitting or idle, it appears that you are intensely discouraged due to previous failures. If the tailor appears to be measuring you to stitch your clothes, it means you will hear fruitful news in the very near future, but if he tells you that he cannot stitch your clothes, it means that you will have financial as well as social problems in the very near future unless you move to correct your situation. If the tailor tells you that your clothes are ready, it is a favorable sign of either a promotion or further success for you. Any form of argument, quarrel, or violence with a tailor spells your irresponsible behavior towards life.

b. You are a tailor: A good dream suggesting you are finally on your way towards a better future. If you have someone assisting you, it means you can trust any of your friends around you.

TALKING. Depending to whom and how you are talking, an interpretation can be had.

a. You are talking: If you appear talking loudly and in an angry mood to anyone, it denotes a setback due to your acutely nervous disposition. But if you speak loudly and with delight, it means that you may either inherit a good amount or you may expect financial assistance. If you appear to be speaking very softly, it means that you are not sure of your next step in life. If you appear talking to family members, you may essentially derive some benefit from them. Talking to businessmen presages better days ahead, while talking to friends means you will embark on a short but fruitful trip. Talking to your spouse foretells the imminent arrival of guests. Attacking anyone verbally while talking underscores your tendency to stay isolated.

TAXI. A taxi symbolizes a short journey. Depending on your situation vis-à-vis the taxi, other significances could be had.

a. You and a taxi: Hailing a taxi symbolizes your desires to get things done fast and consequently it reflects your character as hasty. Entering one denotes the imminency of your journey that you have been waiting for. If the taxi driver tells you that your trip will be difficult, it is a direct prophecy denoting hardships in your way but if he does not say anything and continues towards your destination, it means that sooner or later things will turn to your favor. Coming out of a taxi heralds the end of a successful project whose fruit you will enjoy very soon. Driving around in a taxi with no particular reason symbolizes your desires to achieve greater success.

TEA. Tea symbolizes financial loss and an unhappy period marked by quarrels and arguments.

a. You and tea: Making tea reflects a nervous and an unhappy nature. Drinking tea alone signifies an impending financial loss due to your own faults while drinking tea with friends or business partners means others have been responsible for your failures in life. Drinking tea with your parents means a tense period within the family while with your spouse, it means petty arguments may lead to quarrels and even a short-lived separation.

b. You are invited for tea: Being invited for tea in a dream is a good sign, for it foretells pleasant surprises, which may change your life for the better.

TEACHER. A teacher symbolizes caution and patience.

a. You see a teacher: If he or she happens to be your current teacher, it is a sign asking you to take great care in your daily affairs. A teacher's presence also asks you to desist from any unlawful act. If you see your teacher of your school days, it is a good sign, telling you that patience on your part will finally bear fruits.

b. You are a teacher: A good sign promising a positive result to your labors. It also means that your belief in modesty is better than having unrealistic dreams.

TEARS. Tears symbolize happiness, joy, and a dignified life.

a. You are in tears: If you are unhappy and in despair, happy and joyous moments are near. If you are poverty-stricken, you will have enough to live a contented and a dignified life. If you have minor ailments, you will be fully cured within forty days.

b. Others are in tears: If you see your parents in tears, you will have a life free from any potential danger. If it is your spouse, it denotes a perfect harmony. If it is your children, you will always have harmony at home.

TEETH. Teeth, depending on their situation, symbolize favorable as well as unfavorable developments.

a. You and your teeth: If you dream of your teeth falling off by themselves one by one, it suggests that you will exchange a greedy and a vicious life for a spiritual one. But if you dream of a single tooth either being extracted or falling off, it means that you will lose a very important friend due to your own folly. If a tooth falls off through violence and you bleed profusely, the dream has no prophetic significance. Dirty or discolored teeth signify ill health although temporary, while if they appear in perfect condition, it means you will continue to have good health and if ailing, at least a partial recovery is in sight. If you see several teeth lying around you, it is a warning to be careful in your moves. Seeing teeth of other people in whatever form warns you to beware of tricks against you.

TELEGRAM. A telegram essentially foretells good and pleasant news.

a. You receive a telegram: If it is from your parents, you will receive help in some way or the other. From employers, it denotes promotion, or if unemployed, perhaps a job proposal. From a business partner, it suggests modest financial gains, while from friends it presages an invitation where you will benefit. From cousins or distant family members, it suggests a calmness of mind. If you do not identify the sender, you are in for a pleasant surprise. If someone tells you that you have a telegram, it means that you will have a positive response to your desires.

b. You send a telegram: Sending a telegram denotes your ability to exercise control over your mental and emotional faculties. A telegram of condolence, whether you receive it or send it, symbolizes the beginning of a good period.

TELEPHONE. Depending on the situation and the subject discussed on the telephone, several interpretations can be had.

a. You and a telephone: If you appear to be in the act of telephoning a friend or a family member, it means that you will shortly meet with despair due to faulty planning. But it will be short-lived through your own efforts. But if it is to your parents and if you appear to ask help, it underscores your present unhappy period. If they console you, it is an assurance that eventual help will come through the interventions of others. If they appear to chide you over your situation, it indicates no help is in sight unless you move yourself. If the

189

telephone conversation circulates over exchange of greetings, it means that your situation is not as bad as you think. If your parents praise you through a call, it means you are quite cautious in your approach to life. If someone calls and threatens you and you do happen to recognize that person, it is a warning to be careful, but if you do not recognize that person, it means to be prudent and beware of jealous persons around you. If someone asks you to telephone a certain person on his or her behalf, it is a sure sign to disregard advice of persons pretending to be friends. If someone tells you that there is a telephone call from someone for you and that you have to answer the call immediately, the interpretation depends on the situation. If you happen to find the telephone that bears the caller, it means that very soon you will discover "things" hidden from you for a long time and if you happen to be "searching" for the telephone that bears the call either in the house, office, or elsewhere and you fail to find or see the telephone of which the person informed you, it means several persons are trying to harm you but do not have the courage to do so, since you have not done anything unlawful. If your wife or children telephone you, no matter what the subject discussed may be, whether pleasant or otherwise, it shows the great importance you attach to your family. If you happen to telephone them, the bonds appear yet stronger.

TENT. A tent symbolizes a timely help and relief from hardships and miseries. It also symbolizes a temporary halt to a bitter and a stormy period.

a. You are in a tent: If alone, it indicates a timely help from your present afflictions from a person you least expected. If there are friends or persons whom you do not recognize, it means you will accidentally come across a person or more who will greatly alter your life for the better. If you appear to "see" rain or storm outside the tent with you safely inside, it is a sure sign of some relief through your timely awareness. If the tent happens to tilt or collapse, it means whatever you have been doing is incorrect and unlawful and must hence prepare yourself for legal proceedings. If you rush to correct your ways, problems could be averted. If you see several tents around you, whether occupied or empty, it is a promise of hectic activity, which will be beneficial. Tents being pulled down suggests the end of an idle period while tents in flame presage a change in address much for the better.

b. You are putting up or erecting a tent: Putting up a tent alone suggests hard and serious efforts have to be made to acquire the most modest standard of living. If you appear to be helped, your path to success would be greatly eased, thanks to compassionate friends around you.

THORN. Thorns symbolize obstacles and problems due to one's negligence and irresponsibility.

a. You see thorns: Just seeing thorns is a warning to refrain from building unrealistic goals in life. If you appear to be very near a bush full of thorns, it foretells obstacles unless you become realistic and responsible.

b. You are hurt by thorns: If you "feel" hurt, it suggests a calm period however temporary, but if you "bleed," it is a sign of loss due to negligence. It is also a warning to choose reliable friends.

THUNDER. Depending on the loudness (supposed distance) of the noise of thunder and your situation, several interpretations can be had.

a. You hear thunder: If you hear thunder nearby (a loud report), it is a good sign, symbolizing the beginning of a new era in your life. If someone tells you that he heard thunder, it means the end of misunderstandings and animosities with your former friends. If the noise is faint, which means the thunder is at a distance, it is an ominous sign, signifying despondency, ill health, and a sad atmosphere in the house. If you have recently had any quarrel with your spouse, practice restraint or else your relations will worsen.

TORCH. A torch, depending on its situation and yours, has several significances, both favorable as well as otherwise.

a. You and a torch: A flaming torch in your hands presages honors and respect due to your thoughtful acts in the society. If while holding the torch the light suddenly goes off, it means temptations, if uncontrolled, could ruin your life. But if you happen to intentionally put off the light, it suggests the fruition of your projects within the next one hundred days. If you happen to light the torch, it is a clear sign of your determination to carry on your profession, which will sooner or later be crowned with success much to your joy. If someone attempts to prevent you from lighting the torch, whether he succeeds or not, it means jealous persons around you will make a futile attempt to harm you.

b. You are handed a torch: If it is flaming or with some light, it foretells riches through inheritance or through lavish gifts. An unlit torch signifies discouragements and obstacles.

TORRENT. A torrent symbolizes difficulties and financial loss. It also symbolizes misunderstandings and quarrels within a family. As such, it is considered an unfavorable dream.

a. You see a torrent: Just seeing a swollen river with overflowing waters rushing wildly is a warning to immediately refrain from risky business undertakings. If you appear to see property being destroyed or taken away by the torrent, it forebodes difficulties that you could overcome only through thoughtful thinking.

b. You are caught in a torrent: An embarrassing dream suggesting lawsuits against you. But if you manage to save yourself, the probabilities of you committing fallacies that would eventually create a lawsuit against you will be reduced.

TOWER. A tower symbolizes courage, determination, and honesty. It also symbolizes a delayed realization of your ambitions.

a. You and a tower: If you happen to pass a tower, stand near it, or see it from a short distance, it is a reassurance of the continued courage within you to have faith in yourself. Entering a tower underscores your desire to achieve your goals through fair means. A red-brick tower promises the realization of your goals but with some embarrassing delay. A semi-ruined tower reminds you that "all is not yet lost" and encourages you to have hope. A fully damaged or totally ruined tower means a temporary setback but one that you could overcome with a correct presence of mind.

b. You climb a tower: Climbing with ease to reach the top promises success if your goals are modest, while if you appear to have difficulty or appear not to gain any height, it is again a sign of delayed success. If you appear frightened while climbing the tower, the dream has no prophetic significance.

TRAIN. Among the several dozens of dreams that signify success, and end to despondency, despair, and a bad period, a modest success in business and financial affairs, reunion with family and in general an end to a bad period, perhaps the train in a dream could rank as the foremost of them all.

a. You, the train and the tracks: A moving goods train suggests an appreciable gain in business if approached with care while a stationary one asks you to prepare to venture into the world of trade and business, since it would be to your benefit. A passenger train in "full steam" presages a very beneficial meeting, which will greatly influence your future. If you happen to be seated in the train, it is advised to maintain your calm, since sooner or later things will turn to your benefit although you do not seem to feel the advantageous situation you have. If you happen to see a moving passenger train with no passenger in sight, it means you must seriously rethink the degree of confidence that you have so far placed in others. A goods train at the station is a sign of a small business success while a passenger train at the station heralds the arrival of friends. But if you are waiting to board a train at the station, it signifies a short journey not exceeding a few hours, which may not be of significant value. Any type of train derailed warns of impending losses due to carelessness. If while in a train you happen to see tracks running parallel to the train you are riding in, it is a sign of support from friends or family members. If you see the tracks suddenly go towards a different direction, a short period of uneasiness is presaged but which will not have any serious effects on you. And if while riding a train you see a train passing by in the other direction, it is a promising sign of a reunion with your estranged spouse, a sudden reunion of siblings and other family members. If you appear to be nearing a station, it means an imminent business meeting. If you happen to board a train at a station with ease, it underscores your realistic approach to life and if you find difficulty, it suggests a slight alteration in your ways will greatly reward you. If dining or eating something in a train either alone or with friends, it denotes your satisfaction with your present affairs. Riding in a train through a desert means new horizons and opportunities will be soon available to you. Riding through a city or a village means you will suddenly come across an old friend, while riding through a jungle or wooded area reminds you of the need to settle certain outstanding matters, which if left unresolved will be a source of continued annoyance.

TRAP. A trap symbolizes unhappy developments in one's life. As such, it is considered an unfavorable dream.

a. You see a trap: Whether in the form of a hole or a metal trap, it is a serious warning to be strictly aware of what is going around you. If there is a live animal in the trap, it is a good sign, signifying there is still hope to extricate yourself from your present woes by thinking sagaciously. If you see a dead animal in the trap, it is a sign foretelling "friends" around you will ultimately be the main cause of your problems. Think wisely and act carefully!

b. You are laying a trap: Laying a trap for others is an unfavorable sign, since it reflects your vicious character, which should be mended. If you find yourself trapped, it forebodes legal problems.

TRAVELLING. Depending on the reasons for your travel, several significances can be had.

a. You and travel: If you are travelling as if fleeing from friends, family members, or from home, it forebodes quarrels due to excess nervousness. If fleeing from your children, it means you have been too passive in tackling your problems. Travelling on business or pleasure means things will ultimately be in your favor. Have patience.

b. You travel with others: Travelling with your spouse, children, or family members symbolizes a happy life free from complications. With your employer it means a promotion.

TREASURE. Treasures in a dream have favorable as well as unfavorable significances. Depending on the situation and you, several interpretations can be had.

a. You see or come across a treasure: If you suddenly stumble on a treasure, it denotes enough wealth through inheritance. If you appear to be "hunting or searching" for treasure and you come across one, it denotes a sudden and unexpected business deal (only if you are a businessman) in the near future that will bring you appreciable gain. If someone tells you that he or she has found a treasure, it means that you will gain the benefits of a certain person who will greatly enhance your goals in life, but only if they are in harmony with the laws of the land.

b. You see others with treasures: If you see others digging for treasures, it is a sign of encouragement. If you see them quarreling over an object (and if you are a businessman with partners), it presages a dispute with them, which may eventually lead to violence. If at work, you may experience disputes with your co-workers unless you sagaciously tackle your situation. Restraint, sagacity, and wisdom are strongly advocated.

TREES. Trees, depending on their appearance and type, symbolize growth, prosperity, emotions, and ability.

a. You see a tree: A well-foliaged fruit tree with unripe fruits symbolizes expansion of business or trade, dependable friends, and good children, while with ripe fruits it suggests achievement of your goals sooner or later. A bare tree speaks of an isolated life and a bitter married life. A flowering tree denotes the ability within you to achieve your goals, however difficult they appear to you. Any type of palm tree foretells beneficial trips. A fir tree suggests continued good health; an oak tree symbolizes strength and health, a calm life, and a good spouse. If any of these trees appear withered, it forebodes a difficult period marked by poverty and unhappiness. A walnut tree in any situation signifies loss, quarrels, and even violence. A yew tree symbolizes good luck in general. A dead tree underscores your worries for the past and hence reminds you to look to the future.

b. You climb a tree: Being in the act of climbing a tree with ease denotes success while finding difficulty to do so suggests your weakness in facing the realities of life. Falling from a tree denotes your careless behavior. If someone asks you to climb a tree and you accept, it means in the very near future you will receive an employment opportunity that may drastically change your life. If you refuse to do so, it means that you are indifferent to the developments around you and care the least even for your own future.

TUNNEL. Depending on the situation, a tunnel symbolizes hope, a temporary setback, and even a state of uncertainty.

a. You see a tunnel: Just seeing the mouth or entrance of a dark tunnel foretells a general setback although temporary, while if lit, it means there are several chances for you to solve and overcome your problems, but with determination.

b. You are inside a tunnel: If you find yourself inside a dark tunnel, your acquaintances will be the chief cause of your worries. If you appear frightened and lost, it forebodes uncertainties due to incorrect planning. But if you see a light or an exit, be it even at a distance, it means persons whom you least expect will intervene to solve your difficulties.

TURBAN. A turban symbolizes deceit, hypocrisy, bloodshed, and misery.

a. You see a turban: A black turban warns you to strictly beware of potential criminals and opportunists masquerading as either friends or innocent people. If you happen to touch the person wearing the black turban, it means you will soon fall victim to deceit and hypocrisy that will bring you untold miseries. A white turban symbolizes false promises, while a multi-colored one foretells a happy event. If you happen to wear a black or white turban, it means that you are gradually entering the world of sins and crimes. If a person with a black turban promises you happiness, it is a direct prophecy of bloodshed and fratricidal hatred.

U

UMBRELLA. Depending on the position and the situation of it, an umbrella symbolizes hope, hopelessness, financial gains and loss. It also symbolizes protection from harm.

a. You and an umbrella: An umbrella lying on the floor signifies the hopelessness within you while an upright or leaning on the wall signifies hope. Holding an open umbrella under the rain foretells financial gains and also underscores your careful disposition. An open umbrella held under normal weather reflects the falsehood within you. If someone else happens to hold an umbrella over you regardless of whether it is raining or shining strongly, it is a sure sign of financial help and moral consolation from an acquaintance. Being presented with an umbrella from anyone signifies protection from harm while if you appear to present it to someone, it is a sign of a modest financial gain within the next forty days. Buying an umbrella suggests your awareness in life, while forgetting it temporarily foretells a modest gift from a family member. To appear to lose your umbrella and to appear searching for it endlessly symbolizes a financial loss, although not very much. Finding yourself in a shop or a place where there are several umbrellas means good support from family members. If you see yourself either being attacked or attacking someone with an umbrella, it means that you will not have any form of support from family members and hence such a dream serves as a reminder that you have to face the rigors of life alone. Breaking an umbrella spells your hopelessness.

UNCLE. An uncle in a dream symbolizes encouragement and support.

a. You see your uncle: A good sign of consolation if you are afflicted with worries. If your uncle gives you a present or foretells good days for you, it is a direct prophecy that it will come true. If you appear to present your uncle with something or appear to be involved in a friendly conversation, it means you will prosper no matter how the odds appear against you for the moment.

b. You visit your uncle: A wonderful dream suggesting you are unawaredly on the threshold of success. Inviting him spells the end of all your worries.

UNDRESSING. The significances of undressing in a dream rests solely on the reasons. Accordingly, several significances can be had.

a. You are undressing: Undressing at home or in private suggests a life full of failure while undressing in public forebodes grave problems arising out of your past errors. Undressing a child to redress him again signifies a constructive insight, while undressing a woman (by a man) reflects a lack of understanding towards the realities of life. If you (a woman) appear to be forcibly undressed by any man, it is a warning to beware of your next step or face a terrible financial loss and social problems.

b. You see others undressing: To see others undressing forebodes bankruptcy (for a businessman) and illness for the ordinary.

UNHAPPINESS. Unhappiness, contrary to what it implies, symbolizes joy, success, and friendly relations with all.

a. You feel unhappy: If you dream you are unhappy for a certain reason that has been haunting you in the conscious state, it is an indication that patience will ultimately relieve you from that burden. If it is unhappiness due to illness, unemployment, or some other form of misunderstanding that you "feel" about it in your dream, it is an assuring sign that they will ameliorate progressively.

UNIFORM. Depending on what uniform one wears, several interpretations, both favorable and otherwise, can be had.

a. You and the uniform: If in the conscious state your profession compels you to wear one and you see yourself in that uniform (non-military), it means a continued modest life, but if the uniform appears torn or dirty, it foretells continued hardships until you aggressively move to mend your ways. A military uniform (if you are a member of the armed forces) means that you are quite content with your present situation and also underscores your desire to remain in the armed forces. If you once wore a military uniform and as a civilian you again dream of wearing one, it means that you are unhappy with your present situation. It also means that you are continually worrying about your past errors although they may have been minor. If you dream someone is presenting you with a uniform (belonging to any organization), it is a good sign promising happier days.

URINATING. Dreaming of urinating in one's dream symbolizes nervousness, fright, and unhappiness. It is often the case that even a mature person may wet his bed if he dreams of urinating, but strictly if he is nervous and in despair.

a. You are urinating: If you appear to be urinating in an open space and in the presence of others, it symbolizes the nervous breakdown within you. If you appear to be urinating in an open space but away from the eyes of the public, it reflects the great fright within you. But if you manage to find a lavatory, it means that you will finally find the legal means to get rid of your present worries. If while dreaming of urinating you actually wet your bed, it means you are not yet ready to face the challenges of life and need counselling.

b. You see others urinating: If you see any person urinating in the open, it speaks of the deep shameless behavior within you, while if in a closed space, it signifies unhappiness within you due to your fickle nature. Any animal seen urinating heralds the end of your worries. If any of your children appear to be urinating on you, it is a sure sign of ingratitude of that particular child and if you see any of them urinating on the ground, it foretells the end of domestic worries. If any person threatens to urinate on you, it is a warning to beware of enemies masquerading as friends.

V

VAGABOND. A vagabond symbolizes a carefree life devoid of any particular ambition. He also symbolizes loss, dishonor, and fraud.

a. You are a vagabond: If you (a woman) dream of becoming a vagabond, it reflects the dishonorable behavior within you vis-à-vis your present or former husband. If you (a man) dream of becoming a vagabond, it is a strong warning to desist from your irresponsible ways in life.

b. You see a vagabond: If the vagabond approaches you without any words or gestures, it means that you have to become very serious and beware of scoundrels. If he gestures or speaks to you, it foretells a sad development, perhaps the loss of a family member. If you in turn speak with him, it foretells uncertainty due to your unrealistic ways in life. If the vagabond gives you something, it forebodes dishonor, but if you give him something without talking to him, it means a sudden change in your life, which will be for the better. Arguing or quarreling with a vagabond but not encouraging or appeasing him means that you will finally have a more positive approach to life.

VALLEY. Depending on the description of the valley and your position, a valley symbolizes prosperity, isolation, unhappiness, and even setbacks.

a. You see a valley: A deep and a barren valley symbolizes the possibilities of entering the world of business, while if it is covered by forest, it suggests success only through hard work. A cultivated valley symbolizes success gained easily and through sheer good luck. A shallow and a barren valley underscores your isolation in society while a shallow but forested valley suggests unhappiness in domestic matters.

b. You are in a valley: If you appear alone in a green valley regardless of its being deep or shallow, it means that you will unaidedly realize the fruits of your labors while if in the company of any other person, you will be generously assisted by friends. If you find yourself in a barren valley either alone or with friends, it means that you will have to replan your next step or face losses from which you may not recover very soon.

VASE. A vase, whether of metal, china, or glass, symbolizes a happy beginning and a happy ending where business and relations are concerned.

a. You see a vase: A large vase symbolizes favorable grounds for a new beginning in life through your own efforts. With flowers it reflects help and encouragement from dependable friends. A normal-looking vase reflects a humble yet a constructive beginning. If with flowers, it means a modest help. A broken or a crushed vase symbolizes a mishap in your plans.

b. You are presented with a vase: Regardless of its size and material and whether with flowers or not, it is a sign of progress in your work, which should spell success in the long run. If your wife presents you a vase, it is a sign of deceit from her part. From your parents it means a happy ending to all your affairs.

c. You present a vase to someone: If you appear to present a vase to any of your family members, it is a good sign, promising a success within the next few months. If to others it means you will realize your ambitions to such an extent that you will be able to help the less fortunate.

VEIL. A veil symbolizes hypocrisy and falsehood.

a. You see someone with a veil: Such a dream warns you to discontinue your relations with doubtful persons. If the veil has an opening or appears torn, you will have ample proof of the conspiracies and the conspirators within forty days.

b. You appear veiled: Such a dream means you are hiding a hypocritical and a fraudulent identity that will be harmful to you. Such a dream also speaks of a lawsuit.

VERSE. Reading or writing a verse symbolizes one's realistic ways in life. It also symbolizes contentment.

a. You and verses: Reading them suggests a well-earned rest while writing them reflects your realistic ways. Correcting or rewriting a previously written verse denotes your ability to change your lifestyle at your will. Writing verses reflects the depth of seriousness within you.

b. You hear verses being read: If it is from any holy book, it symbolizes spiritual growth within you and if it is from a poetry book, it underscores the contentment within you. If someone presents you with a book of verses and you accept, it is a good sign of respect from the society and if you refuse to accept, it means that you are being gradually swayed towards the world of vice.

VILLAGE. A village symbolizes tranquillity and good health.

a. You see a village: If you see a village from a height or distance, it suggests tranquillity within you and friendship with all. Nearby it symbolizes a wonderful married life. An abandoned village symbolizes disappointment.

b. You are in a village: Being in a village reflects your contented behavior. Such a dream also underscores your honest and friendly character. If you happen to speak with a villager, it is a harbinger of a good life.

VINEYARD. Depending on the situation of the vineyard, it symbolizes profits, loss, success, as well as uncertainty.

a. You see a vineyard: A beautifully laid out vineyard full of grapes signifies a sudden financial gain. It also means a fortune through inheritance. A vineyard although green but without grapes foretells uncertainty due to improper planning and a dried-up vineyard suggests loss while a burnt vineyard forebodes bankruptcy.

b. You are in a vineyard: Walking in a vineyard, whether with or without grapes, suggests your ability to think and act constructively only if the required efforts are made. If you appear to be harvesting grapes in the vineyard, it is a sure sign of good fortune. If you happen to be eating grapes there, it is a sure sign of good health and a successful love affair. If you are married, it is an assurance of a happily married life. It also means success in business affairs.

VIOLIN. A violin symbolizes a happy marriage and prosperity.

a. You see a violin: Just seeing a violin foretells a happy period of harmony within the family. Touching a violin or holding it presages an end to misunderstandings between friends. Seeing any family member, a friend, or even someone you recognize play a violin foretells a new love affair or a marriage within the family and if you are already married, there will be a perfect harmony with your spouse. If you do not recognize the person playing the violin, it forebodes sad days, perhaps a financial setback and bickerings within the family.

b. You play a violin: If you appear playing a violin and if you are ill in the conscious state, it means that you will recover soon, much to your own surprise.

VISIT. The significance of a visit in one's dream depends on who is visiting whom. Accordingly, several interpretations can be had.

a. You pay a visit: Visiting a friend in a friendly atmosphere foretells the imminent beginning of a new and a fruitful project. Visiting your parents symbolizes your serious approach to life while a visit to uncles or aunts, paternal or maternal, presages success for you and your family. Visiting a doctor (as a friend) symbolizes your sound health. A visit to your employer as a guest symbolizes success, while if with a request suggests problems at your place of work. A visit to your siblings denotes continued encouragement while a visit to your in-laws suggests continued harmony within the family.

b. You are visited: A visit by your parents reflects the respect you command in the society while a visit from friends and acquaintances foretells small joint business ventures, which will be crowned by success. A visit by a doctor suggests failing health due to negligence.

A visit by aunts and in-laws forebodes a short misunderstanding within the family, which could be resolved through an amicable approach and patience.

W

WALKING. Depending on where, with whom, and how you are walking, several interpretations can be had.

a. You are walking: If you appear to be walking fast as if evading someone, it means you are passing through an uncertain period. Walking at leisure signifies the successful end to a project. Walking on a flat and a deserted stretch foretells an unhealthy and an isolated life in case you continue your uncompromising ways in life. Walking on a green space or in the countryside signifies good health, financial success, and friendly relations with all. Walking towards any means of transportation symbolizes the urge within you to change your life.

b. You walk with others: If you appear to be walking with people whom you recognize, it means favorable results to your labors, but essentially through the assistance of friends, and if you do not recognize them, it means that you insist on having blind faith in your own ability that would not be too favorable to your liking in the long run. Walking with your spouse and children means important and constructive decisions will be made soon.

WALL. A wall symbolizes obstacles, an unhappy period, and even lawsuits. As such, any wall is considered as unfavorable in a dream.

a. You see a wall: If you see a wall blocking your path or you appear to be enclosed on all sides by a wall, it foretells obstacles and problems at your place of work or in business. If you appear to stand idle or hopeless against a wall, it suggests a bitter period marked with unhappiness at home and continued misunderstanding with friends. If you appear to be climbing a wall, it reflects a strong urge to conquer your problems.

WANDERING. The significance of wandering depends on what the mood is and the feelings within you at the time.

a. You are wandering: If you are despondent, unemployed, and in an acutely unhappy mood, it means you will sagaciously tackle your problems. Although the results will not be in your favor, you will feel comparatively satisfied within the next forty days. If you are already contented in your conscious state and you appear wandering, it means that you are a voracious and a greedy person. Practice modesty, which will gain you total satisfaction.

WAR. Contrary to what it implies, war symbolizes peace, happiness, and friendship.

a. You hear about war: If you hear war has been declared between two or more countries, it is a sign of calm and peace coupled with happy moments within your family. If you dream that two or more countries are already in a state of war, it foretells success and prosperity.

b. You see war: Seeing war with action and even the dead but without blood symbolizes a rebirth in you in which you will have all the possibilities to begin a more meaningful life. However, signs of blood eliminate any prophetic significance to the dream.

WAREHOUSE. This is a dream for the businessman. Depending on your situation vis-à-vis the warehouse, various significances can be had.

a. You and a warehouse: If in despair and in bankruptcy, the sight of a warehouse promises a return to better days. If well off, it promises further gains.

b. You are in a warehouse: If you (a businessman) appear to be walking in a warehouse and if you are satisfied with the way your wares are being stored, it signifies a big profit, thanks to your philanthropic ways in life.

WATER. Water symbolizes good health, success, and a good spouse together with average riches.

a. You see water: A clear expanse of water symbolizes good health with a modest-to-good future free from any danger. If the water appears dirty or muddy, it reflects an unclear or somewhat evil intention within you. Clear flowing water symbolizes the possibilities of exploiting positive forces within you while if unclear, it denotes deviation from a normal life.

b. You are in water: If you happen to be in a clear or potable expanse of water, it symbolizes a successful love affair leading to a good marriage. If you are in a dirty or a muddy expanse of water, it symbolizes continued quarrels with family members and friends. Drinking clear water indicates an early recovery from a minor ailment. It also suggests a partial end to your major problems. Drinking muddy or unclear water forebodes an illness, although short-lived.

WEALTH. Wealth, if in large amount, symbolizes misfortune and total bankruptcy. For the poor it symbolizes petty gains.

a. You and wealth: If you are modestly rich or even poor in your conscious state and you dream of being suddenly wealthy or having gained immense riches, it means that you will have the benefit one day to have the minimum means of life, but if you are rich and already wealthy and you dream of having further wealth and if you feel satisfied, it forebodes loss due to greed and undesired risks. Practice modesty.

WELL. A well symbolizes loss and problems arising out of past errors.

a. You see a well: Just seeing a well reminds you not to indulge in any untoward act, since the outcome would be grave. If you appear to see water in a well, there are chances that you would finally come to your senses and forego any harmful activity, but if the well appears to be dry, it denotes that you will have to answer acts that you have committed against the society in general.

b. You are in a well: If you appear to be in a dry well, it means that you and no other person is responsible for your bitter days while if you dream of being in a well with water where you can drown, it means that you will have a bitter period marked by imprisonment. But if someone appears to come to your rescue, it is a sure sign that in the conscious state a Samaritan will help you.

WHIP. A whip denotes anger, temper, and revenge. As such, it is considered an unfavorable dream.

a. You and a whip: Holding a whip in your hand symbolizes the intense anger within you, while using it on someone reflects the animosity you hold for a certain person for a long period. Practice tolerance. If you are being whipped, it means that you are lazy and must become more active in case you desire to taste the fruits of your life. If you attack the person who is whipping you, it means a last-minute effort by you will greatly help in developing your life.

WHISTLING. Whistling in one's dream suggests an early end to a hard period. Whistling to attract the attention of an animal, a bird, or a human being has no significance.

a. You are whistling: Whistling to some musical tunes or songs signifies the fact that you are still unaware of the success that you are already having. If in the conscious state you happen to be deeply sad, it means that very soon you will have your share of joy.

b. Others are whistling: If you see others whistling, it means others will benefit from your folly. Refrain from permitting others to use you as a tool and think and plan wisely.

WIDOW. This dream has no significance for a man. Depending on your situation and the circumstances, various significances both favorable as well as otherwise can be had. In general, her presence is considered ominous. It must be borne in mind that only if the widow is recognized is there a significance to the dream.

a. You and a widow: If you are planning to marry very soon and you see a widow, it means a small misunderstanding with your future spouse could spark a major crisis. If just before the marriage ceremony, the widow tells you that you will have a bad period, it means you will face several small problems, which you could resolve with sagacity. If you are already married and she tells you so, it means you have to beware of jealous persons around you. If she invites you to dine and you accept, it means in the future you will have an invitation where you will dislike the atmosphere. If she threatens or chides you and if you react boldly, it means you will contain your problems through wisdom.

WIFE. A wife symbolizes courage and support. Her presence also symbolizes calm and tranquillity. An untrustworthy wife is discounted.

a. You and your wife with whom you share cordial relations: If you are sick and if your wife tells you that you will recover, it is a sure sign of recovery although partial. If you are unhappy and in despair, her presence is a sign of courage. If she comforts you, it means within a week you will find happiness. If you are in prison and you dream of your wife, her presence symbolizes a form of relief, since your term may be reduced. If you have a case against you, either you will win it or the sentence would be very light. If you are unemployed and your wife consoles you, although you may not get employment immediately, her presence greatly lessens your torments.

b. You see your wife whom you doubt: If you have unfriendly relations with her in the conscious state because of doubting her integrity or her character and if you dream of her, you must consider whatever she says as false.

WINDOW. A window symbolizes feelings, status, and possibilities.

a. You and a window: If you approach an open window in a room, it means that you will gain further respect and status in society and if someone appears to open it for you, it means there are several chances and possibilities waiting for you. If the window appears half-open, it denotes a tense period of bickerings. If closed it suggests a temporary halt to your social activities, but if you open it wide, it means that you will regain your lost status as a result of jealousies.

If you happen to see out of the window and you see someone friendly approaching you, it means new helpful friends and if someone happens to throw an object at you while you are gazing out of the window, it betokens conspiracies against you. A broken or shattered window reflects your angry nature. Practice calm.

WINE. Wine has several significances depending on the situation in general.

a. You see people drinking wine: If you see yourself drinking wine with friends, it is a sign of success in your modest goals while drinking alone forebodes domestic strife and loss chiefly to your wife's incorrect ways. But seeing people drinking wine means you are too lethargic. Such a dream also means that while others have been having success in life, you have been living in a fool's paradise. If someone invites you to drink wine, it means that very soon you will meet with at least an appreciable success in your life. If someone appears to throw wine on you in a friendly gesture, it means you will have every reason to celebrate a success within the next few weeks.

WITCH. A witch symbolizes an end to major problems. It also symbolizes reconciliation within the family. At the same time, a witch's presence also symbolizes quarrels and jealousies.

a. You and a witch: Seeing any female individual whom you may consider as a witch means you must expect some developments whose outcome cannot be guessed. But if the witch approaches you and exchanges a word of greeting or asks whether she could be of any help or asks you what your needs are, it is a sure sign that the majority of your problems will virtually vanish much to your satisfaction. If the witch gives you something (rare in a dream), it means a financial gain, a help, or an expensive gift from a quarter you least expect. If you argue with a witch, attack her, or threaten her, it forebodes quarrels with your friends. It also means jealousies against you. If you dream you are a witch or someone tells you that you look like a witch, it means that you have the potential within you to be more useful to yourself and the society.

WOMAN. A woman, young or old, beautiful or ugly, symbolizes negative developments whose consequences will turn out to be very grave.

a. You see a woman: If you (a married woman) see a woman whom you recognize but do not share any form of relations with her and if she tells you that she is interested in forging friendship with you, it means you are heading for a collision with your husband unless you rush to examine your situation with your husband. If she invites you for tea or dinner, it is a sure sign of quarrel with your in-laws. If she criticizes your husband or children, it reflects the complete concord at home. If she presents you with something and you accept the gift, it is a sign of financial setbacks for you and your husband. If you refuse to accept her gift, it means you are content with your situation. If you (an unmarried woman or a divorcée or a widow) see a woman and if she talks, makes gestures, invites you, or attempts to gain your friendship, and if you refuse to either answer her questions or her proposals, it means that you are on your way in life and you will reap the fruits of your labors sooner or later. If you behave the opposite, it means continued worries and problems will get the upper hand on you. If you (a married or an unmarried man) see a woman and whether you recognize her or not, whether you have animosity with her or even if you may have cordial relations with her, any form of argument, contradictions, and threats suggest a tense period where you will become more agitated at the slightest worry. In general, her presence is ominous and reflects deceit and calumny against you.

WOUNDS. Depending on the place of the wound, several significances can be noted.

a. You and the wound: A wound on the abdomen symbolizes a short-lived illness while a wound on any hand symbolizes a short-lived halt or rather an impasse to your social and economic activities. A wound on the chest signifies a successful love affair, which will end in marriage. A wound on the lower part of the body (thighs or feet) signifies a temporary halt to your business travels while a wound on the stomach suggests you are getting too greedy in your search for more wealth. Any wound on the knees symbolizes a financial loss, while on the navel, it signifies business success. Any wound on the back part of the body symbolizes jealousies and conspiracies by those very persons whom you have been considering trusted friends.

WREATH. A wreath symbolizes the burying of the past and ushering in new and fruitful activities. It also symbolizes the end of a bitter cycle in one's life.

a. You see wreaths: If you see several of them in a shop or being made, it signifies the sudden end of a terrible cycle in your life. If you are told that you can have one of them, it signifies a wonderful love affair that will drastically change your life. If you take it, there is every indication that your new love affair will be to your absolute satisfaction. If you see yourself with a wreath in your hand or appear to carry one as if in a funeral procession, it means that you will personally solve all your problems without the least assistance of others. It also speaks of your determination to bury and forget the past. If you appear to be laying a wreath on a grave and whether you recognize the dead person or not, it is a sure sign of a new life much better than you expected, thanks to your timely awakening.

WRITING. Depending on what and to whom something is written, several interpretations can be had.

a. You are writing: Writing letters signifies good news, hope, and support for you. Writing a text or a manuscript symbolizes your patience and at the same time sadness within you. If you see others writing, it means an unexpected timely intervention to help you.

Part Two
Nature in Your Dreams

ANIMALS

BAT. A bat symbolizes conspiracies and a general setback. It also symbolizes ill health and quarrels. An ominous dream indeed.
A flying bat speaks of conspiracies against you. A bat roosting symbolizes a short period of unhappiness. If fallen on the ground, it means a modest financial loss. A dead bat speaks of a general setback. A bat flying past you foretells a short spell of illness. A bat appearing to attack you speaks of an impending quarrel with friends. Killing a bat in one's dream signifies a determination to isolate yourself from undesired individuals around you.

BEAR. A bear in a dream is often associated with animosity and revenge. It is also a symbol of ungratefulness.
If the bear appears menacing to an extent of having frightened you, such a dream warns of impending problems through indecent acquaintances. If the bear attacks you, it denotes your enemies are busily conspiring against you. If you manage to frighten away the beast, your enemies will fail in their plots against you. If you shoot, kill, or even wound the beast, it signifies your desires to change your way of life for the better. A docile or a friendly bear, near you or at a distance, warns you to beware of hypocrites around you.

BULL. A bull signifies prosperity, success, health, and courage.
If you see a bull grazing, it means you are headed for prosperity. If you find yourself near the animal in a peaceful atmosphere, it is a sign of encouragement to go ahead with your plans. If you appear to be feeding the animal, it is a sign of good health, and if you happen to be ailing, it is a sign of at least a partial recovery. A dead bull in one's dream underscores your nervous and hesitant behavior. A slaughtered bull means a business success and perhaps a celebration. If you dream of riding a bull, it means a sudden financial gain, though not too much.

CAMEL. A camel is a symbol of patience and reward.
Just seeing a camel near or far reminds you to continue your labors

until you are crowned with success. If the animal appears to be feeding, it is a warning to prepare yourself for a difficult though temporary period of hardship. If the animal appears to threaten or even attack you, it foretells a temporary disappointment in business deals. If the animal appears to near you, it means you have the support of friends. A slaughtered camel symbolizes happiness within your family. A dead camel speaks about futile conspiracies. Riding a camel or seeing several of them means a fruitful journey.

CAT. A cat symbolizes deceit, unfaithfulness, and hypocrisy.
If the cat appears sleeping, it speaks of deceit and conspiracies by those very persons you consider friends. If a cat happens to scratch you, it speaks of your spouse's unfaithfulness and if it bites you, it denotes ingrate children. If the cat appears friendly, it betokens lies and slanders against you by your own family members. A dead cat signifies an end to mental torture.

COW. A cow is a symbol of satisfaction, good health, and affection.
If a cow appears to be grazing, it underscores your satisfaction with life. If a cow is frightened of your presence and runs away, it means you must change your character in order to attract good friends. If a cow nears you and shows her affection, it means you will continue to have a happy married life if married, and if unmarried, a good spouse awaits you. If you appear to be feeding a cow, it means continued respect from friends and family members. A cow licking you suggests good health and recovery for those in ill health. A dead cow foretells an impending financial loss through sheer carelessness. A calf in a dream indicates new possibilities to make full use of your talents. A slaughtered cow underscores the great degree of nervousness within you.

DEER. A deer symbolizes hesitation, fright, and affection.
If you see a deer running, it emphasizes your hesitation in making decisions. If a deer appears to be frightened and runs away at seeing you, it underscores the fright you have harbored within you as a result of your untoward acts in life. If a deer approaches you, it underscores your honest behavior and foretells success. A dead deer speaks of undependable friends. If you successfully hunt a deer, it foretells better times ahead for you. Several of these animals, either

216

grazing, standing, or even running, signifies a gradual rise in your social and financial status.

DOG. A dog symbolizes friendship, faithfulness, and truth.
If you dream of your dog that is already dead, it underscores your compassionate and fiercely incorruptible nature. If you see your dog (which is alive), it means you will very soon receive some valuable help from a friend. If you see a strange dog, you will soon befriend a good person. If the strange dog appears menacing, it speaks of minor misunderstandings between friends. A dead dog speaks about dashed hopes. Attempting to kill or even hurt a dog foretells deep misunderstandings leading to quarrels within your family. If you find yourself amidst several dogs and if you do not feel frightened, it means you will soon gain your wish if modest. It also means good news, if you are waiting for results of any project.

DONKEY. A donkey symbolizes wisdom and simplicity.
If a donkey appears to near you, it means you will receive valuable advice and perhaps adequate help to start an independent life. If you happen to ride the donkey, it speaks of your reticence and sagacious nature, which will ultimately be rewarded with modest gains. If a donkey appears to attack you, it means you have not been careful enough in your planning. A dead donkey means you have been unrealistic.

ELEPHANT. Just like a donkey, the elephant also symbolizes wisdom. An elephant also symbolizes prosperity and truth.
If the elephant nears you harmlessly, it underscores your balance of mind, wisdom, and care. If you happen to ride the elephant, it means success through honest and hard work, ultimately leading to prosperity. If the elephant appears to be trumpeting or raising its trunk, you will arrive at your goals, even if it takes time. If you appear to be speaking to an elephant, it means you are blessed with the courage to uphold truth in life, no matter what the consequences may be.

FOX. A fox symbolizes a wily and an unashamed nature. It also symbolizes malice.
If the fox nears you or threatens you, it suggests that those acquain-

tances whom you still consider friends are busily conspiring against you. If you appear to chase away the animal, you will have an undisturbed domestic life. A dead fox signals the futile nature of those trying to harm you. If you shoot or kill a fox, you will successfully neutralize malicious rumors spread against you.

FROG. A frog symbolizes prosperity, a good harvest, health, recovery, a favorable court verdict, a happy married life, and an end to disputes between friends.

A frog swimming indicates prosperity in business or a promotion at work. A frog on an elevation signifies a good harvest or success in agricultural activities if you are a farmer. A frog jumping into the water promises a fair court verdict, usually in your favor. Two or more frogs on land or in the water means a happy married life. Mating frogs symbolize an end to misunderstandings between friends. A dead frog underscores your carelessness and indifference to life. Killing or stoning a frog in one's dream denotes a haphazard approach to life.

GIRAFFE. A giraffe symbolizes kindness and a humble nature.

If the giraffe appears to be grazing, it means those who have a wrong notion about you will finally understand you. If you appear to be feeding the animal, it underscores your helping nature. If you appear to see several of these animals either at rest or grazing, it means success is there, but after a struggle. If they appear to be very near, it means help from unexpected quarters.

GOAT. A goat symbolizes greed, a loss, and even a sudden financial gain.

If the goat appears to be grazing, it means you are gradually acquiring a taste for greed. If you see a single male goat with large horns on an elevation, it means a sudden financial gain. If the goat is not on an elevation but on the same level as you, it means new ventures will be proposed to you. But if the goat appears to be at a level much below your level, it symbolizes a financial loss, perhaps leading to bankruptcy if you are not careful enough. A dead goat indicates a simple life while a slaughtered one foretells good health within your family and for you in particular.

GORILLA. A gorilla symbolizes idleness, unhappiness, and poverty. A gorilla seen in a forest means an unfruitful life. The animal seen in a cage denotes impending unhappiness arising out of a judicial procedure against you. A gorilla in a zoo (but not caged) foretells unemployment or lack of possibilities for even a modest life. A dead gorilla signifies abject poverty due to your lackadaisical behavior.

HORSE. A horse symbolizes honors, promotion, good business, and stability.
If you appear riding the horse, it means fortune through business. If employed, you will have a promotion. If you appear to give affection to the animal, it signifies trustworthy friends and if the horse "speaks" to you, it means a stable life. If the animal appears to be galloping away, it foretells a break in your love affair or marriage. Buying a horse denotes honors while feeding the animal means continued good health.

HOUND. Hounds symbolize an unending search in life to attain a specific goal whether in spiritualism, politics, or business.
If you see hounds in a hunt, it means hard work is needed to achieve your goals. If you see the hounds attacking the hunt, it suggests that you are nearing your goals at a faster pace. A hound near you foretells political success while feeding them suggests your nearness to spiritual values.

HYENA. A hyena symbolizes greed, conspiracies, and fraud.
If you see a hyena from a distance, it is a warning to disassociate yourself from certain acquaintances before they create harm to you. If the animal appears to devour a dead animal, it signifies great loss and even mental tortures arising from excess confidence in business associates. If you are not in business, it foretells problems at work. Several of them symbolize worries. If you appear to frighten them away, it means your enemies will themselves fade away. Feeding a hyena underscores your tendency towards fraud and greed.

LION. A lion symbolizes authority, justice, and compassion. A lioness symbolizes perseverance and hard work.
If the lion appears roaring, it foretells a sudden promotion at work or a successful business career. If the lion nears you menacingly, it

219

underscores your authoritarian ways in life, but if with a friendly gesture, it means you will prosper with enough riches. If you appear to touch the beast, it underscores your compassionate and philanthropic nature. If you see a lioness from a distance or near, it means encouragement. If the beast appears to roar at you, it is a warning to replan your goals.

MONKEY. A monkey symbolizes uncertainty and falsehood.
If the monkey appears to be sitting calmly, it means that your enemies are conspiring against you. If the monkey appears to threaten you, it is a sign of uncertainty. If you manage to drive away the animal, it is a hopeful sign that your labors will ultimately gain you a modest life. A dead monkey denotes an end to a period of nervousness.

PIG. A pig symbolizes shamelessness and loss.
If you see a pig, it symbolizes sheer bad luck. If planning a journey, an interview, a business venture, or a visit to friends, postpone them for at least a week. If you see two pigs, it speaks of a shameless conspiracy against you due to jealousies. If pigs appear to be enclosed in a pen, it speaks of legal procedures against you.

RABBIT. A rabbit symbolizes ability to make swift decisions. It also symbolizes financial gains.
If the rabbit appears running, it means ability to make swift and timely decisions while if lying down, it means a chance to prove your abilities. Feeding a rabbit means a financial gain.

RAT. Rats symbolize greed, destruction, and animosity. As such, a rat in one's dream is considered unfavorable.
Several rats at any place symbolize your greed to have more of everything even at the cost of breaking the law. Rats in or around the kitchen mean a sudden end to all your constructive aims in life. If seen near the bedroom, it forebodes jealousies and enmity. If you manage to chase away the rat or even kill it, you will triumph over your hardships.

SHEEP. Sheep symbolize inner peace, truth, and friendship. They also mean a contented life.

If you see a sheep or several of them grazing, it means you will finally have inner peace after a stormy period, thanks to your truthfulness. If you find yourself among the sheep, it means your friends will not disappoint you. If you appear to give affection to a sheep, it speaks of your content in life, and if a sheep approaches you with a friendly gesture, it speaks of support from your friends. A lamb symbolizes grateful children.

TIGER. A tiger symbolizes mean and ungrateful behavior.
If a tiger approaches you menacingly, it is a warning to keep away from those of whom you have the least suspicion, since the result could be violence. If a tiger appears to attack you, it means deep misunderstandings with your friends, but if you manage to frighten it away, you will be able to rid yourself of undesired acquaintances. A tiger in a cage underscores your careful behavior.

TOAD. A toad symbolizes evil temptations and an urge towards dishonesty.
Seeing a toad nearby means a strong temptation lies within you to indulge in dishonest means to achieve your goals. Refrain from sin. From far away, the power of temptation weakens. If you kill the toad or see a dead one, it underscores the ability within you to resist the urge.

WOLF. A wolf symbolizes greed, voracity, and treachery. As such it is considered an unfavorable dream.
Just seeing a wolf in a dream is said to bring bad luck. If a wolf approaches you, whether menacingly or otherwise, it means that the person whom till today you have considered to be your most trustworthy friend will ultimately turn out to be your worst enemy. If you manage to kill the beast or at least frighten it away, you will be saved from false slanders and accusations.

ZEBRA. A zebra symbolizes an uncertain future.
If the animal appears grazing or at rest, it means certain forces will urge you to enter a trade that will ultimately lead you to misery. If the animal is seen running, it means a sudden change in your life, for the better or for the worse. A herd at a distance or nearby suggests a stormy period, which you will have to face with careful planning.

A dead zebra is said to suggest the end of a bad period in life and the beginning of financial and social gains.

BIRDS

BLACKBIRD. A blackbird is considered as the herald of poverty, affliction, and even death. As such this bird in a dream is considered as ominous.

Seeing one perched near your residence warns you of impending torments, either from unemployment, financial difficulties, or a bad spouse. The bird perched on or around your window presages a violent death within your family and one lying dead or killed around your house forebodes an untimely death of a youth in the family.

CHICKEN. A chicken symbolizes realization of goals, good health, and prosperity.

If the chicken appears to be feeding, it is a good sign that your labors will reach fruition, though with a little delay. Several of these young ones seen with their mother (a hen) promise sudden and unexpected financial gain, either through inheritance or through an accidental meeting with a person who will simply like to make you rich. A chicken on your body suggests extremely good health. A dead chicken suggests a temporary setback, but if you appear to "lay to rest" the chicken, the results of the setback will be minimized.

COCK (a rooster or a bantam). A cock symbolizes unnecessary problems created through one's rashness. It also symbolizes rivalry between business partners and jealousy among friends.

A cock perched lazily signifies rashness and uncontrolled anger while one that crows while perched warns you of impending misunderstanding between business partners or friends that may turn into a bitter feud. If it crows while on the ground, it indicates violence between lovers caused by sheer jealousy. A dead cock or one killed to be eaten suggests an end to a difficult period.

CROW. A crow has both good and bad significances. It symbolizes longevity and good health and also quarrels and unhappiness, depending on its situation in the dream. Strangely, it also symbolizes justice.

If the crow appears sitting alone, it symbolizes a long life with good health. If several crows appear to quarrel with each other while trying to devour a dead reptile or bird, it denotes deep misunderstandings within the family for a certain period but which will ameliorate later. If you see several crows together in what appears similar to a "session for judicial deliberation," you will ultimately receive justice in your life. A dead crow symbolizes a long period of difficulties coupled with bad health. A crow in flight means a short journey.

DOVE. A dove symbolizes peace, affection, and kindness.

A pair of doves means a happy married life. A single dove is a symbol of your incorruptible ways of life. Several doves in flight signify your unending love and affection for the poverty-stricken while a single one in flight suggests your ability to prosper without aid. A dead dove is a warning not to deviate from your spiritual leanings. If you appear near to a dove, it signifies you will have inner calm and peace.

DUCKS. Ducks symbolize harmony and happiness in a family.

Ducks swimming symbolize a happy atmosphere in your home. Ducks in flight symbolize a long and a prosperous journey. A single duck in flight suggests uncertainty to your projects while a dead one foretells a misunderstanding with your spouse.

EAGLE. An eagle symbolizes high aspirations and goals in life. It also means a dominant tendency. It also symbolizes uncertainty.

If the eagle appears flying in circles, well above in the sky, it suggests uncertainty, and hence advocates a more realistic approach to life. If the eagle appears to fly in a particular direction, it speaks of the one particular goal that you have and hence suggests at least a partial belated success. If the eagle appears to be sitting on a cliff, an elevation, or a tree, it underscores your domineering nature. A dead eagle means you have to fully replan your lofty plans.

OSTRICH. An ostrich symbolizes hypocrisy, worries, and hardships.

If the ostrich appears running wildly, it speaks of dubious friends. If the bird appears standing still, it suggests your inability to arrive at your goals, however modest they are, due to sheer laziness, and hence unhappiness. If you see several of these flightless birds, it suggests unbearable hardships due to your extravagances. A dead ostrich is a sign of relief from worries and hypocrisies.

OWL. A symbol of sagacity and at the same time, according to the situation of the bird, an ill omen. This nocturnal bird is chiefly associated with unbearable miseries.

If you appear to see this bird from a fairly good distance, it symbolizes your sagacious character, which could benefit you if fully and well utilized. But if the bird appears near to you, it speaks of ill health or perhaps a loss of life in the family. A "hooting" owl forebodes death through violence. More than one of these birds around you, if quiet, speaks of an impending tragedy, either financial, acute poverty, or a mental ailment, but not necessarily death. A dead owl, however, suggests an end to a bad period.

PARROT. A parrot symbolizes a confused state of mind. It also speaks of an unfruitful life.

If you appear to see parrots in flight, it means you are too confused and need rest. If you see a single parrot either flying or perched on a tree, it suggests uncertainty of your present plans. A speaking parrot symbolizes your awkward and illogical approach to life. A caged parrot means an unfruitful life unless you seriously seek professional assistance. A dead parrot means a temporary peace of mind.

PARTRIDGE. This game bird symbolizes both prosperity and misfortune depending on its situation vis-à-vis yours.

A single partridge at a distance means modest financial gains. Nearby it speaks of general prosperity. A flock of them, either on the ground or in the air, symbolizes a sudden general loss and difficulties. A dead partridge means a general recovery. Hunting partridges speaks of your strong desire to overcome your difficulties through logical solutions. A walking partridge speaks of your indifference to life and society in general.

PEACOCK. A peacock symbolizes false pride and bloated ego. It also symbolizes jealousies and misunderstandings often leading to violence.

If you see a peacock with its wings spread, it underscores your false pride, falsehood, and dishonest dealings in life. If the bird appears to be turning around, it denotes your vain search for fame through illegal means. If it appears to be standing still or even sitting, it speaks of jealousies against you within your own family. If a peacock is with a peahen, it foretells misunderstandings with your spouse. A flying peacock forebodes an impending quarrel within your family while a flying peahen symbolizes the impossibility of realizing your goals.

PELICAN. A pelican symbolizes friendship and human gesture.
One or more pelicans swimming means you can have confidence in your friends. It also means you will find more trustworthy friends. A pelican near you suggests assistance in reaching your goals. Feeding a pelican underscores your human gesture towards those in need. A dead pelican speaks of a temporary social setback due to minor misunderstandings.

PIGEON. Just as a dove, a pigeon symbolizes peace, affection, and kindness. A pigeon also symbolizes satisfactory news.
A pair of pigeons means a happy married life or for the unmarried a good marriage. A pigeon or more around you symbolizes affection and kindness for you from the society. A single pigeon in flight is a harbinger of good news, such as passing an examination, a positive answer to your letter, or a modest success in your efforts. A flock of pigeons in flight is usually associated with a visit from a near friend or family members. A dead pigeon signifies financial loss while a wounded one signifies your continued irresponsibility. If you appear to be feeding pigeons, you will achieve a good percentage of your goals.

SPARROW. A sparrow represents a fickle nature and recklessness.
A flock of these birds in flight underscores your fickle nature while a single one symbolizes uncertainty, at least for the foreseeable future. A dead sparrow heralds the end of a difficult period while a chirping one foretells hardships. But if you appear to be feeding the sparrows, you will have a modest financial gain together with happiness.

SWAN. A swan symbolizes happiness, success in business undertakings, and good health.

A white swan indicates a respectable position in life. It also symbolizes a continued happiness within the family. A black swan symbolizes good health, a good marriage, and good in-laws. If you appear feeding a swan, it signifies an early success. A dead swan underscores your hopeless attitude.

TURKEY. A turkey symbolizes false hopes and deceit.

A cackling turkey warns of indecent acquaintances and asks you to beware of false hopes from them. A standing turkey symbolizes unreliable and dangerous friends. A turkey feeding speaks of conspiracies against you but which will have less effect on you. A dead turkey means you will finally rid yourself of undesirable persons around you. Eating turkey meat means you will overcome your foes peacefully.

VULTURE. A vulture is an ominous symbol. It symbolizes revenge and animosity.

If a vulture appears flying, it is a warning to be on the guard against revengeful persons. If it appears on the ground, it means your enemies are on the verge of harming you, unless you take great care. If the vulture nears you menacingly, it speaks of impending quarrels leading to violence. One or more of these birds feeding warns you to immediately change your way of life or face unfavorable results. A dead vulture means your enemies will themselves fade away. If you appear to kill a vulture, you will triumph over your enemies.

FLOWERS

LILY. Lilies are symbols of honesty and affection.

If you see lilies in a field, it underscores your honest behavior. If you are offered lilies, it suggests you will receive affection from those around you. If you offer the flowers to someone, it reflects your moral values.

ORCHID. Orchid flowers symbolize strong bonds of friendship. For those married it means a happy married life.

If you are presented with orchids by a person you recognize, it symbolizes true and lasting friendship with that person. If your spouse presents them to you, it is a sign of stable marriage. If any of your children happen to present them to you, it means a strong bond of affection between you. If you see a field full of orchids, it suggests an end to hardships, due to intervention of friends.

POPPY. A poppy flower symbolizes deceit, falsehood, and sickness. If you see poppies in a field, it means you are living in a world of deceit and falsehood. If you happen to touch a poppy, it foretells sickness and even death. If you are offered poppies, it means temptations to indulge in sinful and unlawful acts. Beware of what you do.

ROSE. A rose flower (any color) symbolizes true love and deep affection. It also symbolizes a stable and an eventful life.
If you are presented with roses by a person whom you love, it suggests an early marriage. If you buy roses, it means a prosperous business affair awaits you. Cutting rose flowers from the plant suggests a successful end to a project, deserving a celebration.

SUNFLOWER. A sunflower symbolizes a temporary gain, with the following periods not being too favorable.
If you see sunflowers in the field, it means your efforts will be partially successful. If you see a single sunflower, it means a temporary financial gain. If you see dead or drooping sunflowers, it suggests you are planning riches through unlawful means.

VIOLET. A violet is a harbinger of good news. It also symbolizes marriage.
Violet flowers in a field speak of good news. For the unemployed, an employment proposal within a fortnight, and for the sick, an improvement in health. If you appear to hold violet flowers in your hands and if you are unmarried, it means a happy marriage. If you are offered violet flowers and if you are having a difficult period, a sudden general amelioration in life awaits you.

FRUITS

APPLES. An apple symbolizes health, wealth, and happiness.
If you see apples in a basket or elsewhere, it denotes a successful business career. If you happen to eat them, it means a long healthy life. If you appear picking apples from a tree, it means a happy and a stable married life. If you are presented with apples, you will either receive a costly gift or you will have ample help to begin a business. If you buy apples, it means you will have visitors whose presence will greatly enhance your success. Rotten apples denote a short period of uneasiness with your family members.

APRICOTS. Apricots symbolize a happy married life. As such, they have a prophetic significance for the unmarried only.
If you see apricots, it means you will soon find a suitable partner. If you have one, it strengthens the possibility to marry soon. If you appear to be eating apricots, it means you will marry within one year. If you buy apricots, it underscores your desire to exit from isolation. Picking apricots reflects your positive pride in life.

BANANAS. Bananas symbolize a modest and a contented life.
Buying bananas denotes your refusal to look towards higher horizons in life. Eating them reflects your modest ways. Seeing bananas symbolizes an isolated life. Offering bananas to guests or friends underscores the honesty within you. Plucking (raw) bananas bolsters the fact of your reticent and careful nature.

DATES. Dates symbolize spiritual values and an indifference to materialism.
Buying dates underscores your inner urge to maintain your spiritual values. Selling them tells of your desire to forego wealth and materialism. Eating dates symbolizes hard work and honesty. Seeing people pick dates or you picking them is a sign of a successful journey.

FIGS. This fruit is associated with excellent health, inheritance, and a happy married life.
Eating figs denotes excellent health. Being offered figs speaks of a possible inheritance. A plate full of figs signifies a happy married

life. For those dating, it promises an early marriage. Rotten figs symbolize continuous problems within the family. Picking figs from a tree denotes unexpected modest gains.

GRAPES. Grapes symbolize success in love and in business. They are also a sign of continued good health.
If you appear to be eating grapes (any color), it foretells success in love, and as a result, a happy marriage. Drinking grape juice signifies continued good health. Picking grapes from a vineyard indicates the beginning of a prosperous period. Buying grapes signals an end to a bad period. Rotten grapes speak of a temporary financial setback.

LEMON. A lemon symbolizes a bitter period. It also means disputes and deep misunderstandings in the family, especially between those married.
Eating lemons in a dream symbolizes a bitter period marked by continued quarrels within the family, especially between those married. It also foretells a short period of illness. Dreaming about a basket full of lemons indicates a host of problems. Buying lemons reflects the restlessness within you. Lemons on a tree speak of deep misunderstanding between husband and wife. Cutting or squeezing lemon juice underscores an angry disposition.

ORANGE. An orange has both good as well as bad significance in one's dream. This fruit also symbolizes a dramatic change in one's life and also symbolizes illness, judicial procedure, financial loss, and even bankruptcy.
A basket full of oranges indicates a dramatic change in one's life, either for the better or otherwise. But if you happen to trample them or throw them away, you will get rid of their bad effects. If you buy oranges, it foretells illness. If you eat them, it forebodes violence leading to judicial procedures. If you are presented oranges, it means a financial loss and perhaps bankruptcy. If you happen to be eating oranges with your spouse, it foretells deep misunderstanding, often leading to a separation or even a divorce. Oranges on a tree speak of falsehood in love.

PEACHES. Peaches, contrary to oranges, symbolize good health, a stable marriage, and success in your profession.

Eating, buying, or selling this fruit speaks of good health, happiness within the family, and a stable married life. Being offered peaches indicates a generous helping hand from family members and even friends. A tree full of peaches signifies a strong degree of unity within the family. Plucking the fruits from a tree underscores the great importance you attach to your health.

PLUMS. Plums have a good as well as an unfavorable significance. Depending on the situation, an interpretation can be made.

A plate full of plums signifies good health, whereas rotten ones signify illness within the family. Buying plums indicates a forthcoming misunderstanding within the family. Selling plums spells recovery from illness. Picking plums reflects your obstinate behavior.

POMEGRANATES. The ancient Persians considered and we still consider pomegranates in a dream as an ultimate in everything good. As such, this fruit in one's dream is considered propitious.

Eating this fruit denotes a long and a healthy life. Offering them to friends or receiving them means a successful life in virtually all domains. Buying them means an exceptionally good marriage. A basket or plate full of this exotic fruit means plenty of riches and even inheritance of wealth. Picking them from a tree signifies a unique yet a modest life.

RASPBERRIES. This fruit is usually associated with disappointments, quarrels, and misunderstandings.

Eating, seeing, and buying this fruit means a disappointment in marriage, a loss in business, and perhaps bankruptcy. Being offered this fruit symbolizes deep misunderstandings within the family. Rotten raspberries speak of a terrible disappointment for those in love. Picking raspberries underscores your reckless and rash behavior. It also speaks of your refusal to accept any responsibility.

STRAWBERRIES. This beautiful fruit symbolizes true friendship, good health, and a modest yet dignified life.

A plate or basket full of this fruit means trustworthy and dependable friends. Eating strawberries denotes good health. Buying them or serving them signifies a modest and a dignified life. Rotten strawberries mean you are not utilizing all your efforts to reach your goals. Strawberries in a field symbolize a dignified life free from any legal affair.

INSECTS

ANT. Ants symbolize perseverance, a contented life, abhorrence of vice, and a spiritual approach to life. These noble insects also symbolize truth and honesty.

A line of ants symbolizes perseverance and contentment with a modest life. It also promises an ultimate in happiness. An ant carrying a grain or a dead insect symbolizes a life free of vice with spiritual leanings. A flying ant symbolizes a fruitful journey although not with financial gains. An ant hill symbolizes an expansion in your trade. A dead ant means rivals are out to harm you. A lonely ant is a symbol of encouragement. If you happen to hold an ant in your hand, it underscores your honest and truthful behavior. If you find yourself killing one ant or more, it underscores a revengeful character within you.

BEE. Bees, like ants, symbolize perseverance, truth, and even prosperity.

If you see bees near their hive, it speaks of gains through continued perseverance. If you see bees on a flower, it underscores your faithfulness to your spouse. A single bee, either flying or on the honeycomb, symbolizes prosperity. A dead bee means you have leanings towards a perverted mind. Killing a bee means you have an impatient mind.

COCKROACH. A cockroach symbolizes perversion, loss, fraud, and ill health. It is also a symbol of continued family feuds.

Seeing a cockroach or touching one underscores perversion and vice within you. One or more of this insect on the ground foretells ill health while flying cockroaches speak of a disastrous journey. These insects on the wall denote family feuds. A dead cockroach means an end to your present problems. Killing a cockroach indicates your will to mend your ways in life.

CRICKET. This insect is a harbinger of good news. It also suggests a sudden change in your life for the better with spiritual gains.

Seeing a cricket on the grass, ground, or in your home foretells good news, probably a help from a friend or a stranger whom you will meet in the future. A flight of crickets suggests a dramatic change in your life, chiefly for the better. A cricket in your hands denotes a spiritual gain, which will have a fundamental change in your life. A cricket approaching you suggests a modest life. Killing this insect means ill health coupled with a bad period.

FLY. A fly symbolizes greed, vice, and ill health.

Seeing a fly underscores your greedy nature. One or more of these insects on your body forebodes ill health. Several of them on the ground or elsewhere means you have an inclination towards vice and fraud.

SNAIL. A snail symbolizes irrelevance, laziness, and a fickle nature. It also symbolizes the receiving of news, the nature of it depending on the situation of the snail.

A crawling snail symbolizes irrelevance and laziness. A snail inside its shell speaks of a fickle nature. Several snails crawling together speak of good news while a dead one means very disappointing news is on its way. Eating snails means better days after a long period of hardships.

SPIDER. A spider symbolizes protection from harm. It also symbolizes an encouragement towards a righteous path of life.

A spider in the act of spinning a web foretells extraction from a very difficult situation. It also means a favorable verdict in case you have a judicial procedure against you. A spider hanging from a point of its web signifies calm after a stormy period while a spider within the web signifies protection from an impending harm. Two spiders or more together is a sign of encouragement to begin a righteous path in life. A dead spider signals a warning to immediately discontinue impious ways in life. Killing a spider in one's dream means the dreamer is devoid of a logical and a realistic approach to life.

WASP. A wasp symbolizes a short period of unhappiness caused by conspiracies and slanders by those whom you consider to be friends. It also forebodes depression caused by malicious news.

One or more of these insects seen in a dream warn you to control your feelings and wisely tackle those whom you suspect. A wasp menacing you at close range, or even stinging you, signals the beginning of malicious news spread against you either by your own family members or acquaintances that could cause you mental worries. Killing a wasp in one's dream symbolizes a peaceful exit from the clutches of undesired persons around you.

REPTILES

ALLIGATOR (or a crocodile). An alligator or a crocodile symbolizes deceit, unfaithfulness in love, and an impending misunderstanding within the family.

If one or more of these creatures are seen on land, they speak of deceit and unfaithfulness in love. If in the water, they symbolize futile conspiracies due to jealousies against you. If an alligator approaches you menacingly, it denotes petty arguments within the family will lead to deep misunderstandings. But if the reptile harmlessly passes by you, the tense period will be short and will end in satisfaction for all. An alligator in the zoo means a timely intervention by friends to lessen the problems confronting you.

LIZARD. A lizard symbolizes hypocrisy, enmity, and indifference to life. It also symbolizes a temporary business setback.

One or more of these reptiles speak of a hypocritical relation that those whom you consider friends share with you. It also symbolizes a gradual increase of animosity between you and them. A lizard quite near you underscores your indifference to life. Killing a lizard reflects your desire to ultimately begin a new life. A dead lizard speaks of futile conspiracies against you.

SNAKE. Snakes symbolize deceit and treachery through one's own friends and acquaintances. At the same time, depending on the situation of the snake and you it symbolizes health recovery, energy, and sudden financial gains.

Several snakes seen crawling together symbolize a concerted attempt to dishonor you by your own acquaintances. A single snake crawling means treachery in love. A single snake dangerously approaching you speaks of an attempt to physically eliminate you. If you manage to kill the reptile or even frighten it away, you will manage to neutralize a terrible development against you. A dead snake signifies a sudden end to your miseries. A single king cobra symbolizes vast riches through inheritance, but only if it stares at you in the eyes. Holding a snake means the immediate recovery from minor ailments and a partial recovery for acute illness. A snake that appears to harmlessly rest on your shoulders or arms denotes sudden energy, even if you are in old age. Large snakes such as a boa, anaconda, or a python have various significances. Any of them, if threatening, mean strong opposition to your goals. If friendly and even playful to you or to others around you, it means strong support from powerful friends. A kiss from any of these large snakes promises immense financial gains that you least expect. Seeing any of these reptiles coiled up signifies the time is ripe for you to begin formulating your plans, only if lawful.

TORTOISE. A tortoise symbolizes honesty, good health, and a dignified life.
Seeing one tortoise or more underscores your determination to remain true and honest vis-à-vis your own conscience till the end of your life. Feeding one or playing with it foretells a long and a healthy life. Lifting one or carrying it indicates a modest and a dignified life. A dead tortoise reminds you to resist evil temptations that could lead you away from your original goals and aspirations in life.

VEGETABLES

BEANS. Whether fresh or dried and of any color, beans symbolize a difficult period, financial loss, and quarrels.
Eating beans symbolizes difficulties and sickness. Cooking them foretells unemployment and financial loss. Picking them betokens quarrels. Buying them forebodes domestic problems. Selling or throwing them away signifies the lessening of woes.

CABBAGE. Cabbage symbolizes good health, success in one's profession, a happy married life, and friendly relations.
Eating it denotes good health, while cooking it means support from the family. Buying it signifies success is in sight. Offering it or being offered it denotes a successful love affair or a good marriage. It also underscores your friendly nature.

CARROTS. A carrot symbolizes hardships coupled with poverty.
Eating carrots betokens bleak days due to excessive laziness. Drinking carrot juice forebodes financial problems. Buying carrots presages homelessness while picking or harvesting them means much has to be done to achieve the minimum.

CUCUMBERS. Cucumbers symbolize good health, perseverance, and honesty.
Eating them denotes good health. For those acutely ill, it foretells a partial recovery. Buying them symbolizes your perseverance and offering them reflects your honesty. Picking them reflects your determination to evade vice.

GARLIC. Garlic symbolizes health, recovery, and the continuation of good health.
Eating, buying, offering, and being offered garlic in one's dream presages a prompt recovery of those ailing, while if not ailing, it promises continued good health. Picking fresh garlic bulbs speaks of a happy development ahead of you.

MUSHROOMS. Mushrooms in one's dream symbolize a sudden change or development for the better.
If you see mushrooms all over you, it is an encouragement to execute your plans if conforming to the laws of the land. Gathering them indicates an appreciable financial gain, which will materialize through your hard work. Eating them indicates a hasty approach to life and hence one must expect a temporary setback.

ONIONS. Onions symbolize grief and a long period of unhappiness.
Eating or just seeing onions foretells a sad development within the family, ending in grief and tears. Buying them means petty quarrels that could lead to deep misunderstandings. Peeling them means

continuous arguments leading to unbearable unhappiness. Rotten onions indicate an appreciable relief from present sorrows. Harvesting onions reflects your responsibility for your present difficult situation.

PEPPERS. Fresh peppers of any size or color symbolize good health, financial gains, promotion, and a friendly relation with all.
Eating peppers symbolizes continued good health. Growing them indicates a successful business, while harvesting them foretells either a promotion in your work (if employed) or a likeable proposal (if unemployed). Buying them means an early realization of your goals while selling them denotes continued friendly relations with all. Rotten peppers mean temporary problems.

POTATOES. Potatoes have a favorable as well as unfavorable significance in one's dream. Depending on their situation vis-a-vis yours, an interpretation can be derived.
A field of unharvested potatoes symbolizes uncertainty while harvested potatoes on the field mean a modest financial gain. Buying, selling, eating, offering, and being offered either cooked or uncooked potatoes suggests a loss in business and also foretells hardships. Throwing away cooked or uncooked potatoes suggests a partial amelioration to one's problems.

TOMATOES. Tomatoes symbolize good health, good news, and an end to depression.
Seeing a field full of tomatoes symbolizes continued good health while eating them suggests recovery from illness. Picking tomatoes reflects your urge to better your life. Buying tomatoes signifies good news is on the way, perhaps a positive reply to your requests. Being offered tomatoes indicates trustworthy friends will come to your rescue in the hour of need. Offering or selling tomatoes underscores your determination to start a fully new life.